Paul's
Early Letters:

from hope, through faith, to love

Paul's Early Letters:

from hope, through faith, to love

Paul Wrightman

ALBA · HOUSE   NEW · YORK

SOCIETY OF ST. PAUL, 2187 VICTORY BLVD., STATEN ISLAND, NEW YORK 10314

Library of Congress Cataloging in Publication Data

Wrightman, Paul.
   Paul's early letters.

   1. Bible. N.T. Epistles of Paul—Criticism,
interpretation, etc. I. Title.
BS2650.2.W74   1983   227'.06   83-7126
ISBN 0-8189-0440-2

Nihil Obstat:
Garrett Fitzgerald, S.J., S.T.L.
Censor Deputatus

Imprimatur:
† Joseph T. O'Keefe, D.D.
Vicar-General, Archdiocese of New York
May 29, 1983

The Nihil Obstat and Imprimatur are
a declaration that a book or pamphlet is considered
to be free from doctrinal or moral error. It is not implied
that those who have granted the Nihil Obstat and
Imprimatur agree with the contents,
opinions or statements expressed.

Designed, printed and bound in the United States of
America by the Fathers and Brothers of the
Society of St. Paul, 2187 Victory Boulevard,
Staten Island, New York 10314, as part of their
communications apostolate.

---

1 2 3 4 5 6 7 8 9 (Current Printing: first digit)

---

*I would like to dedicate this, my first book,
to those persons who are first in my life:
Elizabeth
James, John, Bridey*

Contents

Introduction

St. Paul's letters are currently enjoying an unprecedented revival of interest within Roman Catholic circles. Not so long ago Paul was presented in caricature—and avoided—as being too "Protestant." It was said, for example, that he exalted faith over works, and was thus dangerous to the "Catholic" position. Today, with several decades of solid Catholic biblical scholarship behind us, we know that, far from being in tension with Catholic faith and practice, the writings of St. Paul actually contain the roots of many of our dearest Catholic doctrines.

To study Paul's letters is to explore the wellsprings of such significant articles of faith as the Communion of Saints, bodily resurrection, and the Real Presence of Christ in the Eucharist. To read through the table of contents of this book is to become aware of the tremendous number of topics about which Paul wrote, topics which will be developed in depth in the text. The first aim of this book, then, is to enable the reader to investigate some of the biblical roots of our Catholic tradition.

A second goal is to provide the reader with a sketch of one of the Church's greatest dogmatic and moral theologians *in action*. St. Paul was no "ivory tower" thinker. He hammered out his theology in the context of immediate need and biting controversy, always with an eye to the long-range implications of what he was saying. To study St. Paul is to discover the general principles behind the specific applications of his theology. This book will attempt to bring to light these general principles and in the process of doing so, enable the reader to sharpen his or her own deductive theological skills.

Thirdly, and most importantly, this book hopes to invigorate the reader's own friendship with Christ through disclosing something of the depth, intimacy, and mystical ecstasy of Paul's friendship with Jesus. Often in his letters St. Paul invites us to follow his example; taking his advice seriously in the realm of spirituality can be an especially grace-filled way of growing closer to Christ.

The perspective from which this book is written is that of development. Paul's letters will be studied in chronological order so that we can see how his thought and spirituality matured from his middle years to his later ones. In this aspect of adult growth Paul stands as an inspiring model for adult Catholics today. He did not stand still in his understanding and faith, but continually allowed his relationship with Christ to carry him to new insights and deeper trust. The theological and spiritual progression in his letters can give us a helpful pattern for our own continuing growth in faith and understanding. Throughout the course of this book we will witness the main themes of Paul's early letters as they develop from *hope* (the letters to the Thessalonians), through *faith* (the letter to the Galatians), to *love* (the letters to the Corinthians). This journey through Paul's hope, faith, and love can become a personal journey of our own leading *us* to a renewed sense of hope, a deeper faith, and a more abiding love.

SUGGESTIONS ON HOW TO USE THIS BOOK

Although *Paul's Early Letters: from hope, through faith, to love* will stand as a biblical-theological work in its own right, it is designed to be used as a study guide to the scriptural text. For this reason the following process is recommended:

1. Read the introduction to the biblical book which is up for consideration. For example, read the introduction to I Thessalonians on pages 3-4.

2. If possible, read the letter under discussion in its entirety at one sitting. For example, read the entire biblical text of I Thessalonians.

3. Then reread the portion of the letter which will be dealt with in a particular section of the study guide. For example, reread I Thessalonians 1-3.

4. At this point read the corresponding section in the study guide, preferably with an *open Bible*, so that you can refer to specific portions of the biblical text as necessary. For example, read chapter 1: ``Joy and Expectation in the Lord,'' pages 4-8.

5. At the end of each chapter of the study guide, answer the Questions for Personal Reflection/Group Discussion. These questions are most effective if responded to in writing. Most chapters have at least one factual (have I internalized the substance of Paul's thinking?) and one personal (how does what God has to say through Paul apply to me personally?) question. If answered in a notebook, the responses to these questions will make up a powerful spiritual journal.

Unless otherwise noted, the biblical text quoted in this study guide is that of the *New American Bible*. For ease of reference this translation is recommended.

Paul's
Early Letters:

from hope, through faith, to love

I Thessalonians

Introduction

First Thessalonians is the earliest of Paul's letters which has survived in canonical form. He may have written letters to some of the young churches before this, but if he did these have not survived. Paul wrote First Thessalonians from Corinth in the middle of his "Second Missionary Journey" to friends and converts he had made in Thessalonica, the provincial capital of Macedonia.

In response to a God-given vision (see Acts 16:9-10), Paul had taken the decisive step of bringing the Gospel into Europe. He was imprisoned, then run out of town, at the first place he stopped—Philippi. Remaining faithful to his task, he went on to Thessalonica, where "some Jews, a great number of Greeks, and numerous prominent women" (see Acts 17:4) accepted his message. We don't know exactly how long Paul was able to stay in Thesssalonica. We do know that it was long enough for him to establish some close personal ties. Before long, however, the violent opposition of the Jews forced him to leave. He next went to Athens, which was singularly unreceptive to his preaching of the Gospel, then to Corinth, which was responsive to the Good News, and where he remained as a missionary for a year and a half.

We can visualize Paul's anguished curiosity as to what was happening in Thessalonica. Unable to return himself, he sent his disciple Timothy to see how his friends were doing. The report which Timothy brought back was wonderfully positive. Paul wrote this letter—which we can pinpoint to AD 51 with the help of archaeological inscriptions—to share his relief and joy with the Thessalonians. He also used the occasion to develop further his teaching and to answer some questions, based on the report which Timothy had brought back with him.

Chapter 1: Joy and Expectation in the Lord

Please read I Thessalonians 1-3. Paul begins with the proper letter-writing etiquette of his time, stating who is sending the letter, to whom it is addressed, and offering words of greeting (1:1). It was customary to follow the salutation with some words of thanksgiving, praising the recipients of the letter. It is apparent from the length and intensity of this thanksgiving that it is no mere formality on his part, but a heartfelt expression of his affection for the Thessalonians. He is deeply thankful that their lives radiate a strength of faith, an outpouring of love, and a steadfastness of hope which speak eloquently of the reality of their conversion (1:3).

Hope is mentioned last, in a place of emphasis, because it is the virtue with which this letter is concerned most directly. Paul recalls his missionary experience in Thessalonica (1:4-6). He remembers the test to which he himself was put, and the hearty response which the Thessalonians gave to his message, despite the fact that the opposition made it no easier for them to receive the Gospel than it had been for him to deliver it. Because of the intensity of their response and the quality of their lives, beginning churches both within and outside Greece are looking to the church in Thessalonica as an example (1:7-8).

Paul goes on to detail the content of the positive reports which he had been hearing about the Thessalonians (1:9-10). Five things stand out in his summary: (1) the welcome which he and his companions had received, (2) their acceptance of the one true God and their rejection of idolatry, (3) their faith in Jesus as God's Son, (4) their eager anticipation of Jesus' return, and (5) the reality of future judgment. Paul must have been very happy to receive these reports. It was clear from them that the church in Thessalonica had remembered and was acting upon those teachings which he considered to be essential points of the Gospel.

Thessalonica, like all Greek cities at the time, was a center of idolatry. Undoubtedly one of the reasons so many of the Thessalonians were open to the Gospel was that they had already experienced something of the lifelessness of their idols. This lifelessness must have been even more evident as they received Paul's message of a living, present God. For Paul, the crucial testimony to the truth that God is alive is the fact of Jesus' Resurrection. He emphasized the Resurrection in his preaching, since this was the foundational fact of Christianity. Even at this early date—less than twenty years after Christ's death and Resurrection—he calls Jesus "Son," a title describing the unique, and uniquely divine, relationship of Jesus to the Father. This passage (1:9-10) ends on a note of expectancy. The theme of Jesus' return is introduced, a theme to which he will return repeatedly throughout this letter. The context of Christ's return for Christians is first and foremost one of joyful anticipation; the "wrath to come" refers to the judgment which those who reject the Gospel are bringing upon themselves.

Given the disastrous chain of events in Philippi (see Acts 16:16-40) just prior to his coming to Thessalonica, Paul was particularly aware of his human weakness, and his dependency on God (2:1-2). He reminds the Thessalonians of these circumstances to underline the fact that his message is a God-given one, not one of his own devising.

He goes on to deny vigorously certain base motives of which he has been accused, probably by some of the Jewish opposition; who hope to discredit his message in his absence (2:3-13). To understand his defense, we need to know that there were plenty of wandering preachers and teachers in his time, "false prophets," who peddled a bizarre concoction of lies, sexual immorality, and trickery. His opposition was trying to destroy his credibility by claiming that he was just another of these wandering hucksters.

Paul's main defense, in this letter as in others, is threefold: (1) he
appeals to his divine commission (2:3-4, 7a, 12-13), (2) insists on his
intimate relationship with the Thessalonians (2:7b-8, 11), and (3) asks
his readers to remember his blameless conduct while he was with
them (2:5-6, 9-10). He asks his friends at Thessalonica to recall some
specific details of his conduct, among them the fact that, unlike other
itinerant teachers, he worked for his living instead of charging a hefty
fee for his teaching.

The seriousness with which he took his missionary work and the
depth of his love for his converts in Thessalonica helps to explain the
heat of his anger toward those Jews who are trying to destroy his
message (2:14-16). The suffering which the Thessalonian Christians
are undergoing is meaningful because it is the same suffering which
the churches in Judea endured and which Paul himself is experiencing. Again, the "wrath" which he mentions is the fact that those
opposed to the Gospel are in the process of denying themselves
salvation. He is profoundly disappointed at not yet having been able to
visit his Thessalonian friends, and sees this as Satan's doing—Satan,
in his understanding, being a personal, superhuman power of evil
irrevocably hostile to God and those who follow him (2:17-18).

At this point (2:19-20) Paul breaks into a celebration of his joy at
the steadfastness of the Thessalonian church. He calls them the *crown*
of his ministry. His choice of words here—he uses the word for an
athlete's crown of victory rather than a royal crown of status—evokes
the image of a vigorous, and sometimes painful, athletic training
finally climaxing in a glorious triumph. Piling image upon image, he
shares his happiness at being able to offer this crown of the Thessalonian church at the coming of Christ.

The Greek word which he uses for "coming" (*parousia*) refers
to the triumphal procession of a victorious king. By Paul's time, this
word was already in the process of being transformed by the early
Church to mean the triumphal return, or Second Coming, of Jesus.
This was one of the most hope-filled words in the theological vocabu-
lary of the early Church, expressing as it did a wholehearted yearning

for the Lord's return. Jesus' return was seen primarily as a time of overwhelming joy. Joy is certainly Paul's emphasis in this short little section. He can think of nothing more wonderful than experiencing the return of the Lord with his friends in Thessalonica.

Returning to his disappointment at the impossibility of his visiting the Thessalonians in person, Paul finds comfort in the fact that he was able to send them Timothy (3:1-5). He forthrightly shares with them his concern about their perseverance in the midst of persecution. The heartening report which Timothy brought back greatly strengthened Paul in his own suffering (3:6-8). Implicit in the reality of shared consolation which he mentions here is the seed of what will eventually develop into his theology of the Communion of Saints.

Again Paul bursts into thanksgiving (3:9-13). He mentions his prayers for a speedy return to them, and for a healing of certain weaknesses in their faith (he himself will offer some guidance in the remainder of this letter). It is significant that he addresses God as "our Father" in 3:11. This was a much more intimate way of approaching God than the typical Jew of that time would have been comfortable with, and shows the personalizing effect which Paul's relationship with Jesus was having on his relationship with God the Father.

Questions for Personal Reflection/Group Discussion:

1. (a) Have you ever had an experience of introducing someone to Christ and the Church, but of not being able to provide the necessary follow-up?
   (b) How did you feel?
   (c) What did you do?
2. (a) Why were other churches looking to the Church at Thessalonica as an example or model?
   (b) Do you think your parish church could be regarded as a model—why or why not?
   (c) Do you think *you* could be regarded as an example—why or why not?

3. Paul is very direct in his expression of friendship and praise for the community of Christians at Thessalonica. As Christians living in today's world, do you think we appreciate each other enough? If not, what would be some ways of encouraging more active support among Christians for one another?

**Chapter 2:   Christian Morality and Its Motivation;
              Jesus' Return**

Please read I Thessalonians 4-5. The word "now" in 4:1 marks a definite transition; Paul is moving from reminiscence and expectation to exhortation and teaching. His tone is serious. It is noteworthy that he speaks in the name of the *Lord* Jesus. In using the title "Lord" to preface the name Jesus, he is emphasizing Jesus' role as authoritative moral teacher and ruler. Paul derives his authority as apostle and teacher from Jesus' authority. He refers to the moral teaching which the Thessalonians learned from him when he was with them in person, acknowledges their sincere attempt to live this teaching, and asks for an even greater fidelity to Christian morality.

The fact that he once again reminds the Thessalonians (4:2) of his prior instruction to them points to the seriousness with which he undertook his mission to preach and to teach. In this verse, "You know" can also be translated as "You have not forgotten." Through this letter Paul is recalling his Thessalonian friends to an active remembrance of his previous teaching. The preposition "in" contains a strong sense of instrumentality. It can also be translated as "through the authority of." Thus, verse two in its entirety could be translated as "You have not forgotten the instructions we gave you through the authority of the Lord Jesus."

Paul continues, in 4:3, with a specific reminder of his past teaching in the area of sexual morality. His teachings regarding sexuality must have been some of the most difficult teachings for the

Thessalonian Christians to internalize. The Christian community at Thessalonica was predominately Gentile, and in Gentile society at that time and place promiscuity was the rule rather than the exception. The city of Thessalonica was also the center of two highly promiscuous mystery cults. For these reasons it is not hard to see why sexual purity was a doctrine difficult to understand and a commandment nearly impossible to obey. This is the permissive social environment (an environment which influenced the attitudes and actions of the Thessalonian Christians just as our environment influences us) from which Paul challenged his friends to total conversion.

In keeping with his positive tone throughout this entire letter, in 4:3 Paul describes holiness, or sanctification, as a process of growth. The implication here is that holiness is not something which is attained once and for all. Rather, since our holiness is really an expression of God's will, its renewal lies in our renewing our commitment to God's will in our lives. In other words, we grow in holiness as we grow in relationship with God.

Many contemporary writers in the area of religion are making a connection between holiness and wholeness. What they mean by this is that holiness, far from being mere pious feeling, is a formative attitude which guides our actions. Real holiness leads to wholeness— a basic unity between spirit and body which, in turn, leads to a close correspondence between inward attitudes and outward actions. This "modern" insight is really a return to the original insight of St. Paul! For him, holiness naturally expressed itself in wholeness of body. Then—as now—in the context of a sexually permissive society, resisting sexual immorality was an important part of a Christian's call to holiness. Paul saw the Christian's power to respond to this difficult calling not in the realm of willpower, but in God's will as realized in their (and our) relationship with him.

In 4:4-6 Paul describes what holiness means in terms of sexual morality. It means that the Christian will strive for wholeness by respecting his "member" (which can also be translated as "body" or "wife"), and that he will not seek to take advantage of his fellow Christians. A Christian is called to revere his or her own sexuality and that of others.

He concludes this section (4:7-8) by reemphasizing the fact that this call to holiness is not some man-made morality, but *God's* call. As such, the motivating power to live it comes from God in the person of the Holy Spirit, and not from ourselves.

Even in the area of brotherly love—an area in which the Thessalonians excel—Paul challenges them not to rest content, but to make "even greater progress" (4:0-12). Timothy had apparently reported to him that the Thessalonians had a tendency to become lost in longing for the Lord's return. This had led to a certain amount of idle curiosity and just plain idleness. Given this situation, Paul counsels calmness, discreeteness, and a good day's work.

Since his departure, some of the Thessalonian Christians had died. The community was rather shaky on its theology of the Resurrection and of the Second Coming, and erroneously thought that their dead friends could no longer be present to experience the joy of Jesus' return. Thus they grieved unduly. Paul writes to comfort and to clarify in 4:13-17. Faith in Jesus' Resurrection is primary (4:14). It entails a connection between his death and the death of his followers, between his Resurrection and the resurrection of those who believe in him. He will develop this connection between Christ and the Christian into the notion of solidarity and the doctrine of the Communion of Saints/ Mystical Body of Christ in his pastoral (second) letter to the Corinthians. Here he simply states the reality of the connection and does not elaborate.

Speaking authoritatively in 4:15, Paul maintains that the dead will in no way be at a disadvantage when Jesus returns. This is so because when Christ appears the dead will be raised first (4:16); then, together with the living, they will meet Christ (4:17). This is a message of great hope because it emphasizes the reunion of all believers with their Lord.

What about the details: the ''word of command,'' the ''sound of the archangel's voice,'' and ''God's trumpet'' (this is actually a threefold parallelism—three slightly different ways of saying the same thing); what about the clouds, and our meeting Christ ''in the air''?

We need to remember that in this passage Paul was writing in an apocalyptic style—the typically Jewish way of communicating about the ''last things''—using visionary imagery and detail which were not intended to be taken literally. Words could not capture the reality of what an apocalypse was attempting to describe. Thus, while the overall event (in this case the Second Coming) being narrated was believed to be historical (as contrasted to mythological), the specific details (like the clouds and the meeting ''in the air'' mentioned above) were seen as hints, or clues, pointing to a much ''bigger'' reality; a reality so ''big,'' in fact, that words could not contain it—thus the need for images.

The picture we get from the details mentioned here is that at a solemn signal from the Father (the ''word of command,'' ''archangel's voice,'' and ''trumpet'') Jesus will return. Like Roman citizens rushing out of their city to greet their Emperor at the first word of his sighting, Christians will be caught up in a joyous homecoming, a glorious reunion with their Lord.

Ours is not the only age when Christians engage in idle speculations about the date of this event. Less than a generation after the death and Resurrection of Christ, Paul was already having to remind Christians not to waste their time trying to second-guess God on this matter (5:1). What really matters is fidelity to the fundamental values of faith, love, and hope. By abiding in these values the Christian will be well prepared for the return of Christ, whenever he comes.

To bring this matter to a close, Paul challenges the Thessalonians to a proper respect for authority (5:12-13a), and challenges them to internalize in attitude and embody in action a host of Christian values (5:13b-22). Living in this way, the Christian community at Thessalonica will become all that God calls it to become. Paul ends by re-presenting his thought about holiness equaling wholeness in the form of a prophetic blessing (5:23-24), asking for their prayers, requesting that his letter be read to the entire church and, finally, giving his friends a formal benediction.

Questions for Personal Reflection/Group Discussion:

1. (a) What is the connection between holiness and wholeness?
   (b) How have you personally reached greater wholeness in your journey toward greater holiness?
2. In regard to the Second Coming, it is just as important to go far enough as it is to keep from going too far.

   (a) What do you consider to be a balanced approach to Jesus' return?

   (b) What would be some of the pitfalls to avoid on either extreme of this balanced position?

II Thessalonians

Introduction

We do not know the precise timing or circumstances behind Paul's second letter to the Thessalonians. We can surmise that he wrote it within a few months of his first letter, in response to further information he had received regarding certain continuing problems. These problems clustered around some mistaken attitudes and actions concerning Jesus' return. Thus his second letter centers on the Second Coming.

This is a particularly difficult letter for us to understand. Paul is thinking in patterns and using images which are largely unfamiliar to us. For example, in 1:5 what can he possibly mean by implying that the Thessalonians are experiencing persecution and trial "as an expression of God's just judgment"? And what are we to make of the strange imagery surrounding the Second Coming which Paul uses in chapter two?

At such difficult points it is essential to understand the particular text in light of the Bible and Christian tradition *as a whole*. Unless we follow this basic principle of interpreting the part in reference to the whole, our understanding will become hopelessly confused to ourselves and we will become a source of confusion to others.

Chapter 3:   The Second Coming

Please read II Thessalonians.   After a brief greeting (1:1-2), Paul bursts into enthusiastic praise of the Thessalonian Christians (1:3-4).

Their faith and love exhibit continuing growth. They are not resting on previous achievements. This witness is even more impressive considering the fact that it is a witness given under persecution.

As stated in the introduction, 1:5 is a problem. What can Paul mean here?—Certainly *not* that God actively inflicts on people evils such as persecutions and trials. We need to step back and see God's judgment in the larger context of God's will.

Because we know from the Gospel that God is unconditionally loving, we can say that God would never actively will anything but unconditional love toward anyone. God's love seeks relationship—a response of love from us. But for our response to be a real response of love, and not just a programmed response, we have to be able to say no. Real love demands real freedom. This is why God created us with free will.

Not all choose to respond to God's love. Evil is, at root, the outward expression of an inner failure to respond to God's love, based on a person's own free choice. The biblical authors did not make the same distinction which we do between God's will and the will of the individual. They saw *everything* as being directly influenced by God. Thus, Paul could write a passage such as 1:5, which makes it sound as if God himself were sending the persecution, or 2:11-12, which makes it sound as if God were actively causing certain people to reject him. In texts such as these, he is following in the footsteps of passages like Exodus 10:27—"But the Lord made Pharoah obstinate, and he would not let them go."

The tradition of the Church makes a distinction between God's *permissive* will, and God's *active* will, a distinction which the biblical authors did not themselves make. In our fallen world injustices—such as the persecution of the Thessalonians mentioned in 1:5—are, so to speak, evils which God "permits" to exist only so that real freedom and thus real love may also continue to exist. Theology calls this aspect of God's will God's permissive will, being careful to distinguish it from God's active will, which is always unconditional love.

Seen in the context of this larger theological perspective, it is possible to understand this section (1:5-10) as saying that for now God permits certain evils to happen, but that at the Second Coming evil will be overcome completely. The punishment of those who reject the Gospel is simply God's acknowledgment of their own free choice.

In 2:1-2 we learn that some of the Thessalonian Christians had worked themselves up into two unhealthy attitudes concerning Jesus' Second Coming. Based on false information, these people were either preoccupied with or terrified at the prospect of the Lord's return, or both. Each of these attitudes distorts Christian faith by obscuring the primary reality of our present relationship with Jesus through a false emphasis on the future.

Beginning in 2:3, Paul demonstrates that the Second Coming is still a while off, because certain conditions have not yet been met. He is assuming a lot of recall of his previous teaching (2:5), the details of which we, unfortunately, do not have.

Using apocalyptic imagery (word pictures of the end times) with which he was quite familiar as a Jew, Paul outlines the following scenario: There will be a massive turning away from the true God to a "man of lawlessness" (2:3), a person so thoroughly evil that his coming will be the final revelation of evil in the same way that Christ's return will be the final revelation of good (2:4). For now, this person is being held back, or restrained (2:5-6). The full revelation of his Satanic power will usher in the final battle between good and evil, a battle in which the Lord Jesus will be victorious and evil will be vanquished forever (2:7-12).

The history of biblical scholarship has shown how pointless it is to try and identify the "man of lawlessness" and the "restrainer." The "man of lawlessness" has tended to be identified with the current religious or political opponent of the person doing the commenting, and the "restrainer" has tended to be equated with that person's position or party or church. Obviously none of these interpretations have been correct, because the Second Coming hasn't come yet!

Other scholars have suggested that these titles will never literally be filled since, they claim, the early Church wasn't writing history at all, but a theology of history which is true on a symbolic level.

What, then, can we gather and what can't we gather from these passages? On the negative side, we must admit that we simply don't know what to make of the details that Paul gives us. On the positive side, he is handing on authoritative early Christian tradition in recognizing the power of evil, pointing out the struggle between good and evil which has already begun, which will get worse, and which will result in the historical (not merely symbolic) Second Coming of Jesus and the final victory of God.

Concerning the timing of the Second Coming, at first Paul, like the early Church as a whole, looked for Jesus' return at any moment. As he kept having to revise his timetable upwards, it must have dawned on him that the important thing was not so much trying to figure out God's timing, as it was simply being faithful to his present relationship with Jesus. This line of thinking is apparent at the end of 2:10, where he describes those destined for ruin as those who have not opened their hearts to the truth. Opening one's heart to the truth is a process which begins in the present and must remain faithful to the present if one is to have a future. Finally, then, it is not so much a question of the theological and/or historical intelligibility of the apocalyptic imagery which Paul uses in these verses, as it is a question of abiding in our present relationship with the Lord. Paul emphasizes the present because it is here that our relationship with Christ takes place. He sees the present as a continuing call for more complete conversion. Thus, it is faithfulness to our present relationship with Christ which will carry us into a hope-filled future.

As in his first letter to the Thessalonians, thanksgiving is an important minor theme throughout this letter. In 2:13 he gives thanks for the Thessalonians as the "first fruits," the first ingathering, of a rich harvest of believers to come. Often in his letters Paul will precede exhortation with thanksgiving. Here, he gives thanks for their faith

(2:13) before exhorting them to follow carefully his authoritative teaching (2:15).

Note his reference to both oral ("by our word") and written ("by letter") teachings. The process of handing on authoritative teaching, either orally or in written form, together with the content of this teaching, was what the early Church referred to as Tradition. Thus, in the early Church there was no conflict (as there was later to be between Protestants and Catholics) between Scripture (the written Word) and tradition (defined narrowly as oral teaching) because *both* were seen as part of the total Tradition of the Christian community.

Paul asks his friends for their prayers for the success of his missionary efforts (3:1), especially that those opposed to the Gospel may not prevail (3:2). His request for prayer reminds him of God's steadfastness ("the Lord keeps faith"), and he uses this thought as the foundation of his hope for them (3:3-5).

A major problem facing the church at Thessalonica was that certain of its members were refusing to work because they felt so strongly that the Lord would return any day. They lived off the rest of the community while waiting and speculating and, it seems, just generally causing trouble. Paul addresses this problem in 3:6-14. He recalls his own example of working for his living while he was with them (3:7-9), reminding them of his rule that "anyone who would not work should not eat" (3:10) and calling for its re-enforcement. If any persist in doing nothing or in causing trouble, these persons are to be shunned (3:6, 14)—but only for the purpose of awakening their repentance so that they may be brought back into the community (3:15).

Paul closes this letter by blessing them in the name of the "Lord of peace" (3:16), peace meaning the fullness of life—with all its blessings, both spiritual and material—in relationship with God. He authenticates the letter (which had been dictated) with his signature, and gives a solemn benediction in the name of the "Lord Jesus Christ" (3:18).

One wonders if this was as difficult a letter for Paul to write as it is for us to understand! Of course the thought patterns and the imagery came naturally to him. Granting this, however, the message of this letter is still terribly "heavy," focusing as it does on Jesus' return in terms of the continuing struggle between good and evil, and in terms of the final consequences of our choice for the one or the other.

The Thessalonians went through their trials—as we go through ours. For now, these struggles prepare us for the Kingdom. But this is not God's last word. Using traditional Jewish imagery, Paul tells us that when Jesus returns evil will be overcome. In spite of his warlike imagery, we must read these passages in light of the big picture, which is God's unconditional love. We must resist the temptation to see God as vindictive. Jesus will return. And his return will usher in the final destruction of evil as well as the final triumph of good. But we must always remember that Jesus will not arbitrarily choose life for some and death for others. Those who will receive life have already chosen life. Those who will receive death have already chosen death long before the Second Coming.

Questions for Personal Reflection/Group Discussion:

1. How can we reconcile God's judgment with God's unconditional love?
2. What can and what can't we know about the when and how of the Second Coming?
3. How do you feel about the increasing emphasis on the Second Coming in certain Christian circles today?
4. Why is the quality of our *present* relationship with Christ so important?

Galatians

Introduction

Paul's letter to the Galatians is a passionate statement of the decisive role of faith. It is full of the just anger of a missionary whose converts—whom he believes to be secure in their new faith—reconvert as soon as he leaves. The Galatians (most likely, an ethnic group of Gentiles living in southern Asia Minor) had seemingly accepted Paul's message, which stressed faith in Christ's saving life, death, and Resurrection as the only thing necessary for salvation. Shortly after his departure, however, certain "Judaizers"—persons who insisted that it was necessary to follow the Jewish law to be a Christian—infiltrated the Galatian church. Soon he heard that many of the Galatians were claiming that observing the Jewish law was a prerequisite for becoming and remaining a Christian.

Paul was shocked and angry. He knew that if this erroneous position were to prevail—if observing the law were considered just as important as faith in Christ—it would effectively undermine the heart of the Christian message. As soon as anything is put on the same level as God's grace—even if it is God's law—grace itself is undercut. It becomes something which we must earn, rather than a saving relationship in which God invites us to share. Paul's letter to the Galatians speaks to the universal temptation to place the requirements of law above the Good News of the Gospel.

After his letters to the Thessalonians, Galatians is Paul's earliest letter, probably written from Ephesus sometime in 54 or 55. In this letter he addresses a severe crisis in the life of the Christian community. The depth and extent of this crisis warns us to be skeptical of those who idealize the early Church and look backward with expressions like, "It would have been so much simpler to have been a Christian then—everything must have been so much more straightforward." If anything, Paul's letter to the Galatians reveals that the early Church had its share of problems just as potentially devastating as those which face the Church today.

Galatians points to the fact that very early in the life of the Christian community the Church had to face a decisive doctrinal fork in the road. One route read "Salvation through Works" the other "Salvation through Faith." As we shall see in the commentary which follows, the relationship between faith and works is a subtle one. If the accent is placed on works, no matter how good they are, they destroy faith. If the accent is placed on faith, good works follow as a loving response.

According to Paul, Christianity is a matter of relationship. Is our approach to God one of trying to earn or bargain our way into heaven? Or is it one of joyful response in a saving relationship freely given to us by God? His letter to the Galatians demonstrates that our answer to these questions is of more than academic importance.

Chapter 4:　A Doctrinal Milestone in the Life of the Early Church

Please read Galatians 1-2. Paul was angry when he wrote this letter. Instead of his usual words of praise and thanksgiving, he writes a rather formal greeting (1:1-5), then plunges into his main complaint: the Galatians are abandoning the true Gospel for a false gospel (1:6-10). The real Gospel is of divine, rather than of human origin (1:11-12). Before contrasting the one with the other, he uses the story of his own life to authenticate his teaching (1:13-2:14). This is the longest autobiographical account from Paul which we have in the New Testament.

Paul tells us that before he became a follower of Christ he had already made it to the top of the Pharisaic pyramid of learning and observance (1:14). In 1:15-16 he refers to his conversion, an incredibly intense experience which forced him to stop trying to save himself and enabled him to find his salvation in the love of Christ. Luke gives us a more detailed account of his conversion, and of his commissioning as the Apostle of the Gentiles, in Acts 9:1-19.

Although Paul does not give the exact details of time or place, his story reveals that immediately after his conversion he went off to the desert for a private "retreat," that he began his public ministry in Damascus (1:17), that eventually he went to Jerusalem to meet Peter (whom he calls by his Aramaic name, Cephas, in 1:18), and that after his visit with Peter he returned to his homeland (in Asia Minor) to continue to preach the Gospel (1:21).

At this point Paul reintroduces the history of his controversy with the Judaizers (2:1). After more than a dozen years of missionary activity, he returns to Jerusalem for further consultation, this time taking with him two friends, Barnabas, who was circumcised, and Titus, who was not (2:1-2). The presence of Titus was significant because he was an embodiment of the issue at hand: could a Gentile become a Christian without first "becoming a Jew" through circumcision? Paul vigorously maintained that circumcision was not only unnecessary, but—for those who were not already Jewish Christians—it was a perversion of the true Gospel.

Paul's position was hotly contested by an opposing group which insisted on circumcision as a necessary condition for becoming a Christian (2:4). Paul tells us that his position was the one which prevailed (2:3, 5). Peter, James, and John—the leaders of the mother church in Jerusalem—concurred with Paul, acknowledged his authority as an apostle of equal status with themselves, and approved of his missionary outreach to the Gentiles (2:6-9). Notice the reference to the "poor" in 2:10, a clear indication of the concern of the early Church for those in need.

In giving us the foregoing information, Paul has provided us with the background to be able to understand the incident he now relates: Peter's visit to the Christian community at Antioch (2:11-14). This community consisted of both Jewish Christians and Gentile Christians. We can assume that the church at Antioch was already somewhat divided in terms of attitudes toward Jewish law. There were Jewish Christians who thought like Paul and no longer considered themselves bound by Jewish dietary laws (which hold, among other things, that Jews could not eat with Gentiles); there were Gentile Christians who considered the Jewish law superfluous (but who also might be quick to try to add some of their old pagan "laws" to their new faith); there were those, the Judaizers, who insisted that everyone—Gentiles as well as Jews—had to submit to the Jewish law before they could be acknowledged as real Christians.

Peter further complicates this already complicated situation. At first he ate unreservedly with the Gentile Christians (2:12a). This was consistent with the understanding that he, James, and Paul had reached previously in Jerusalem. Then, however, some who stressed the necessity of observing the Jewish law arrived (2:12b). These had been sent by James, always a strong supporter of the law, who had apparently had second thoughts about the wisdom of allowing the Gentile Christians to fraternize with the Jewish Christians.

Caught in a bind, Peter equivocated and stopped eating with the Gentile Christians (2:12b). All the Jewish Christians followed Peter's lead (2:13). Whatever fellowship there had been between Gentile Christians and Jewish Christians was now broken. We can imagine Paul's anger. He was so angry, in fact, that he publicly pointed out Peter's inconsistency and challenged him to return to the Gospel (2:14). We know from the book of Acts (15:1-35) that Paul's challenge carried the day, and that another "council" of the leaders in Jerusalem officially endorsed his position.

Antioch, then, was a decisive test case. Paul spotlights it for the Galatians because they are now experiencing precisely the same problems which he had already worked through in Antioch. At issue here is the heart of the Gospel message: does salvation come from observing the law or through following Christ? He insists that the two are *not* compatible (2:16). We need to understand the irony in this verse. The word "justify" is a legal term which means "to be put right with." Paul is using it in this context as "put right with God." In other words, he is saying that legally we cannot be put right with God by legal observance! Justification, he tells us, comes through faith in Christ. By "faith in Christ" he means a relationship of acceptance and dedication. Salvation, then, springs from friendship with Jesus, not from legal observance.

Paul continues, rather rhetorically, to defend his position (2:17-21). In 2:19 he introduces a thought which, like many of his thoughts in Galatians, he will expand in his letter to the Romans: law, in itself, is self-destructive, because no one is capable of perfectly observing it. The law, in other words, deals death. But it is precisely this process of dying to our own ability to live the law that the life of Christ is able to be born in us (2:19-20). In the two concluding verses of this section (2:20-21), Paul underlines the fact that it is Jesus' sacrificial death and not our futile attempts to live the law—which brings salvation.

Questions for Personal Reflection/Group Discussion:

1. In these two chapters Paul contrasts his approach to God before and after he became a follower of Christ. Before, he was a legalist, trying to earn his way into God's good graces. After, he acted out of the realization that God first loved him in Christ, and that the way to the Father was along the road of this relationship. All of us, in a sense, are legalists of one sort or another before we come to have a personal relationship with God. Paul shares the story of his escape from legalism. What is the story of your escape from legalism?

2. What was the doctrinal significance of the confrontation between Paul and Peter at Antioch?

Chapter 5:   The Meaning of Adoption as Sons of God

Please read Galatians 3-4. In the preceding two chapters (1-2), Paul has argued for the priority of faith over law based on his own personal experience and the history of the controversy between faith and works in the early Church. In these two chapters (3-4), he expands his argument by appealing to the experience of the Galatians themselves, and by using illustrations from Scripture and from legal practice at that time.

Unlike most of his letters, in which Paul talks about a variety of topics, Galatians is a letter with a single theme—the fact that a saving relationship with God cannot be based on what we *do* (slavery to law) but, rather, on who we *are* (adopted sons and daughters) through faith in Christ. The fact that he uses everything at his disposal (experience, history, Scripture, everyday illustrations) to prove his point underlines the seriousness of his message. Indeed, Paul saw the future of the Gospel as at stake.

The thrust of these two chapters is to convince everyone (both Jews and Gentiles) in the Galatian church that they were all legalists of one type or another before they became Christians. Rather than return to pre-Christian observances, Paul pleads with them to wholeheartedly accept their freedom in the Lord. His message speaks to a common human dynamic: it is easier to be a slave than to be free. Having tested true freedom, there is a very real temptation to want to return to the slavery of some legalism. In chapter 3, Paul seeks to recall the Galatians to their senses, back to the true Gospel. He contends with them along two major lines; first, that of their experience; second, that of an argument from history based on Scripture.

First of all, then, he challenges the Galatians to remember their experience as Christians (3:1-5). The church in Galatia had apparently been blessed with certain charismatic manifestations. He asks them if they had received these gifts of the Spirit by following the Jewish law or through faith in the Gospel (3:2b, 5). The answer to this question was obvious: the Spirit was dramatically present to them following their faith-response to the Gospel, *before* the controversy over the law had even come up. Paul's point is that obedience to the Jewish law is superfluous.

At this point (3:6), much in the style of a rabbi, Paul begins to argue from Scripture. The story he uses is that of Abraham, whom the Jews and Jewish Christians considered to be their spiritual father. The broad lines of his argument (3:6-29) are as follows: He cites (3:6) the text in Genesis (Gn 15:6) which says "Abraham put his faith in the Lord, who credited it to him as an act of righteousness." For Paul, this text conclusively proves the priority of faith. Abraham was justified (put in right relationship with God) because of his faith—his acceptance of, trust in, dedication to—the Lord, not because he followed the law. He points out that Abraham lived hundreds of years *before* the advent of the Mosaic Law (3:17). His argument from history parallels his argument from experience. He demonstrates that historically, as well as experientially, faith precedes legal observance as the occasion for a saving relationship with God.

In the course of his discussion Paul considers the nature of the Jewish law in some detail. He calls attention to the fact that, according to its own legislation, the law requires that it be fulfilled in its entirety (3:10b). This, of course, is humanly impossible. The law, then, cannot be instrumental for salvation; all it has the power to do is to convince of sin (3:10a). Salvation must come through another means, and for Paul this other means is faith in the promise and the person of Jesus Christ (3:13).

Positively, the law served as a kind of supervisor until the coming of Christ (3:19, 23-24). Now that Christ has come, people are no longer subject to the law as a kind of mediator between themselves and God; rather, through faith in Christ Jesus a direct, and saving, relationship with God is now possible (3:25-27). Just as Jesus abrogated the sometimes arbitrary distinctions of the law, faith in him creates a new family in which all are fundamentally equal (3:28).

Paul's preceding argument from Scripture was tacitly addressed to his Jewish Christian readers. He hoped to convince them of the secondary status of the law by pointing out the priority of faith in the life of one of the greatest Jewish heroes, Abraham. He now (4:1-7) presents an analogy aimed at the Gentile Christian community.

The basis of Paul's analogy is a familiar illustration from domestic life at that time. In his will, a father would designate a son to be his heir, but only under strictly guarded conditions. These conditions often stipulated that the son be subject to rigorous supervision until a specified age. At the appointed time he would receive his inheritance and become his own master; until that time, however, he was little more than a slave.

Paul uses this example from everyday life to point out a parallel between the orphaned son, who is a "slave" until he comes of age, and the Gentile Christians of Galatia, who likewise were slaves until the coming of Christ (4:1-3). In his previous argument he established that the Jews were slaves to the law. In this analogy he maintains that the Gentiles, while not slaves to the Jewish law, were nonetheless slaves to the "elements of the world" (4:3).

By this phrase Paul covers a multitude of pagan religious notions, including worship of the terrestrial elements (earth, air, fire, water), heavenly bodies, and various kinds of spirits. Such worship led to its own peculiar legalisms, because these spirits, planets, stars, and elements made demands and required propitiation. What he is saying here, in other words, is that just as the Jews had been slaves to their law, the Gentiles had themselves been slaves to other forms of law. Both stood equally in need of the Good News of the Gospel.

In 4:4-5 Paul bursts into an abbreviated, but intense, account of the Gospel. It reads almost like a short creed. The "designated time" in 4:4 refers to the fact that God has a plan. It can also be translated as "fullness of time," with the connotation of preparedness. To paraphrase: "In the fullness of time, when the world had been prepared, God sent forth his Son. . ." The coming of Christ was not accidental or casual; it was the climax of an historical process which included his human birth ("of a woman") and human life ("under the law"). Biblical scholars speak of this process of preparation as ''salvation history.'' The history of salvation could be represented by a time line, beginning with creation, flowing through Abraham and Moses, almost falling away with some of the kings, being picked up again by the prophets, reaching its climax in Christ, and continuing in the Church of today.

In 4:5 Paul proclaims the result of this process: freedom from all law and a revolutionary new relationship with God as sons (and daughters) rather than slaves. He does not mention here *how* this new relationship has come about, but given his previous arguments and analogies, we can infer that it has to do with the fact that Jesus, having lived a sinless life, broke through the curse of the law on sinners.

In relationship with God's Son we become adopted children of the Father. The proof that this kinship is a real one lies in the fact that we are invited to address God as *Abba*, just as Jesus did (4:6). *Abba* is the intimate Aramaic (the form of Hebrew which Jesus spoke) word for father, roughly equivalent to our ''Dad'' or ''Daddy.'' Implied in the privilege of communicating with God in this intimate way is the fact that through Jesus our relationship with God is now a *family* relationship. We are part of God's family!

Paul challenges the Gentile Christians not to return to their former idolatries (4:8-11), and then appeals to the entire Christian community in Galatia (4:12-20). He reminds them of his stay with them and warns them of the dubious motives of those who seek to convert them to a false gospel. He concludes these two chapters by presenting one final argument from Scripture (4:21-31). This argument takes the form of an allegory, the slave woman and her son representing slavery to the law, and the free mother and son representing freedom from the law in Christ.

Question for Personal Reflection/Group Discussion:

1. How might relating to God on the intimate level of a son or daughter change your understanding of God and your experience of relationship with him?

Chapter 6: The Contrast Between Flesh and Spirit Life Styles

Please read Galatians 5-6. Have you ever had the experience of finding something that you thought was good suddenly turn into a serious stumbling block—only to have this same thing become, during a later period, an appropriate expression of where you are as a person?

To a large extent, this is the experience which St. Paul describes in his discussion of law. ("Law," in this context, means any system of works which is supposed to put one right with God.) The movements to which Paul calls attention are these.

First, there is the period when one focuses on the law. One sees it as providing a structure and meaning to one's life without which one would be lost. Eventually, however, comes the shocking realization that there is no way that one can live up to all its demands. The law becomes one's accuser.

At this point (the second, pivotal, stage) some persons admit that they can't make it on their own. They turn to God for help. The centering point of their lives becomes their relationship with Christ.

Soon an amazing thing happens (stage three)—they find that the very relationship which sets them free from the good works of law now enables them to do these good works much more fully than they were able to before.

It was this type of experience which led Paul to speak of law in two conflicting, yet complementary, ways: the first as a self-destructive attempt to earn one's salvation; the second as a fitting response to one's relationship with God.

Paul reminds the Galatians of their freedom in Christ. He challenges them not to return to their previous condition as slaves (5:1). He outlines the choice before them: if they decide to undergo circumcision they are, in effect, placing law before Christ, which is the same as denying Christ (5:2). Moreover, by accepting circumcision they are implicitly submitting to the whole law which, as he has pointed out earlier in this letter, is impossible of fulfillment.

In 5:4 Paul summarizes his position in regard to law; anyone who seeks to earn salvation through observing certain commandments has divorced himself from God's grace in Christ. Notice that once again he has placed the responsibility for rejecting God squarely on our shoulders. It is not a matter of God casting us out, but of our removing ourselves from God's presence. 5:4 discloses his negative attitude toward law as a way of works through which people can supposedly achieve salvation.

In 5:5 Paul abruptly introduces the theme of faith. The suddenness of the transition from law and works in 5:4 to spirit and faith in 5:5 serves to underline the opposition between faith and works as approaches to salvation. He goes on in 5:6 to highlight the overwhelming importance of Christ. He begins his sentence with the preposition "in," which implies "union with." Paul, in other words, is emphasizing relationship with Christ as the primary reality in the Christian life. This relationship is based on faith. Its foremost expression is love. Next to this relationship nothing else matters.

5:5-6 mark a significant transition in Paul's letter. Until this point he has been arguing against law as a salvation surrogate. From this point onward he will also speak of law in a positive sense as an expression of a living relationship with God. What makes possible this transition from a negative to a positive appreciation of law is precisely the faith in Christ which Paul stresses in these two verses.

How typical of this letter that just after a major transition (5:5-6), Paul cannot resist throwing a few more taunts at his enemies (5:7-12), before proceeding to his positive discussion of the place of law in the life of a Christian (5:13-25).

He begins this section (5:13-25) by distinguishing between Christian freedom and worldly freedom. This was a crucial distinction to make, especially for Gentile converts to the faith, who could easily misunderstand Christian talk of freedom as encouraging a return to the self-indulgences of paganism. Paul is quick to make a connection between love and service (5:13b). The implication here is that Christian love, rather than being self-centered, is self-giving. As if to underline this point, he goes on to quote the second great commandment (5:14), which places one's neighbor on a par with oneself.

Perhaps it seems somewhat surprising that Paul is now quoting from the law, after having spent most of his letter denouncing it. Just a few verses earlier (5:4) he bluntly stated that those who looked to law for their salvation had, in effect, lost their salvation. Now (5:14) we find him quoting from the same law which he had rejected earlier.

What seems to be a contradiction can be resolved if we think of his attitude toward the law as comprising three distinct, yet cohesive movements. The first is his overwhelmingly negative evaluation of the law as a pretender to salvation. When the law asserts itself as necessary for salvation it becomes, in effect, an idol. This is the sense of law that he speaks of in Galatians 5:4.

The second movement in Paul's understanding of law is pivotal. This is the fact that salvation is a free gift from God. There is nothing we can do to deserve it. Christ's sacrificial death opens up a whole new relationship between us and God. Through Christ, God adopts us as sons and daughters. In this context, salvation means simply to live out this new relationship.

The third movement flows directly from the second. It is a positive reappraisal of law, or "good works," as an appropriate expression of our relationship with Christ. Paul sees law in this positive sense when he quotes from it in Galatians 5:14.

For him, the question of priority is crucial. Good works are positive if they flow *from* our relationship with Christ. They are idolatrous if they are presumed to lead *to* salvation.

These movements in Paul's thought help to clarify a longstanding tension between Protestants and Catholics concerning the roles of faith and works. Protestantism has tended to emphasize faith, at times forgetting the importance of good works as expressions of faith. Catholicism has tended to emphasize works, at times forgetting the priority of faith. In other words, Protestants have stressed Paul's second movement, while Catholics have underlined the third. Today both traditions are coming to see that faith and works are both important, and that there is really no conflict between them if we follow St. Paul's progression of thought.

We can see that the progression of Paul's thought reflects the substance of his theology. Law, divorced from Christ, attempts to take the place of Christ. In this negative sense law becomes an expression of our hopeless attempt to earn our own salvation. If we shift our emphasis from the law to Christ, however, it is precisely our faith in Christ which enables us to reapproach the law positively. Through Christ the law is transformed into a grace-filled expression of our relationship with God.

As Paul hints in 5:16-18, precisely the same movements are at work in the area of motivation. Left to itself, law is self-destructive. It cannot provide its own motivating power; it can only convince of sin. He calls this vicious entanglement of fallen human nature and law the realm of "flesh." It is a mistake to equate Paul's term "flesh" with the English word "body." "Flesh" describes *both* attitudes and actions in which people see themselves as their own creators. "Flesh," in other words, is the pride-full attitude of self-sufficiency which spills over into the self-centered actions which Paul lists in 5:19-21.

Through the transforming power of our faith-relationship with Christ, the law is freed to take its proper place as an expression of our love for the Lord. In Christ, the accent changes from a law of sin and death to "the law of Christ" (6:2b). *This* law is self-motivating. Paul calls this creative union of Christ, people, and morality the realm of "spirit." It is a mistake to equate his term "spirit" with the English word "spiritual" (meaning non-bodily). "Spirit" describes *both* attitudes and actions in which people see themselves as dependent on God for their being and their fulfillment. The term "spirit" points to relationship with God, a relationship which overflows into the gifts which Paul lists in Galatians 5:22-23.

He concludes this section (5:19-25) by contrasting the works of the flesh with the gifts of the spirit. The two are as different as night from day. The one proceeds from our impossible attempts to save ourselves. It is the self-destructive reality of life lived outside of relationship with God. The other springs from the fertile soil of a life-giving relationship with God. By contrasting the various characteristics of flesh-filled with spirit-filled people, Paul is pointing to the ultimate conclusion of two radically conflicting life styles. One leads to death, the other to further life. As always, the choice of which life style we follow remains our own.

Paul give some practical pointers for living a spirit-filled life style in 6:1-10. These include fraternal admonition (6:1), empathy (6:2), humility (6:3), integrity (6:4-5), generosity (6:6), and perseverance (6:9-10).

The letter is authenticated by him with a few words in his own hand (6:11). He dictated most of his correspondence to a scribe, ending with a few words which he wrote himself, to serve as a type of signature.

It it noteworthy that what he writes personally to the Galatians (6:12-18) is really a summary of the letter as a whole. He reminds his readers of the hypocrisy of his enemies (6:12-13). He stresses the sacrificial death of Christ and the new life which this has made possible (6:14-15). The ''brand marks of Jesus'' which Paul mentions in 6:17 are the numerous sufferings he has endured for the sake of the Gospel. He will have much more to say about these sufferings in his letters to the Corinthians. Finally, he closes with a blessing which encourages the Galatians to remain in the grace of Christ by living in the realm of the spirit (6:18).

In these two concluding chapters of Galatians, Paul presents two contrasting pictures of human life. One is life lived in the ''flesh.'' It is self-centered and self-destructive. The other is life lived in the ''spirit.'' It is Christ-centered and leads to wholeness.

What he has done is to describe the end products of two radically different approaches to God. He sketches a progression from law to sin to flesh, on the one hand, and on the other, a movement from faith to grace to spirit.

Paul could not have outlined the danger of embarking on the path of legalism more strongly. He insists that this self-righteous attempt to save oneself—even if done under the name "Christian"— actually unleashes the power of sin more strongly. Today we may not be tempted to the same false approaches to salvation as were the Galatians. All we have to do, however, is walk into any bookstore and view the shelves of self-help books to realize the premium which our society places on self-attained perfection. While diets and dialogue, jogging and assertiveness training are certainly not wrong in themselves, if we are not watchful they can easily erode our relationship with Christ. In this context Paul's letter to the Galatians is as up-to-date as this morning's paper.

Questions for Personal Reflection/Group Discussion:

1. Describe what Paul means when he uses the word "flesh" and when he uses the word "spirit."
2. How can Paul reject the law in Galatians 5:4,
   > *Any of you who seek your justification in the law have severed yourselves from Christ and fallen from God's favor!*
   yet go on to quote from the law in Galatians 5:14?:
   > *The whole law has found its fulfillment in this one saying: "You shall love your neighbor as yourself."*
3. In your own spiritual life, which have you tended to put first, faith or good works? What does this tell you about the nature of your relationship with God?

I Corinthians

Introduction

Paul founded the church in Corinth on his ``Second Missionary Journey,'' immediately after a rather disastrous attempt at converting Athens (see Acts 17:16-34). His Gospel message, which had been spurned by sophisticated Athens, received a much more favorable hearing in Corinth. At that time Corinth was the capital of the Roman Province of Achaia, an area roughly equivalent to that of modern Greece. Because of its strategic location on a narrow isthmus between the Aegean and Ionian Seas, Corinth was second to none in terms of trade and transportation.

Next to Rome, Corinth was the most cosmopolitan city of the Empire, attracting representatives from every known culture and religion. Idolatry prospered: the patron deity of Corinth was Aphrodite, the godess of love; there were many other temples in the city for various members of the Greek, Roman, and Egyptian pantheons; numerous mystery cults flourished in the environs. For those with more intellectual leanings, one could choose from several Greek philosophical traditions. Quite a few Jews had settled in the city. Two-thirds of the population (estimated by some to be as large as 600,000) were slaves.

Given Corinth's commercial and cosmopolitan nature, it is not surprising to learn that this city also held a reputation for debauchery which was second to none. Indeed, the Greek language reflected this dubious honor by using the name of the city as a verb which meant to live a profligate life, and in equating ``lady of Corinth'' with ``prostitute.''

Acts 18:1-17 gives us some of the details of Paul's missionary activity in Corinth. We know that he worked as a tentmaker, that he carried on his preaching and teaching at the synagogue until being forced out by hostile Jews, that many Gentiles responded to his message, and that he stayed in Corinth for eighteen months. All in all, his efforts in Corinth were surprisingly successful, so successful that he was able to leave Corinth for missionary work in Antioch and Ephesus. This missionary work took him away from Corinth for several years.

While in Ephesus, probably in the year 57, he received word of serious problems with the Corinthian church. His first reaction was in the form of a letter which we no longer have (see I Cor 5:9). He received further reports of problems within the community, as well as a number of questions from the Corinthians themselves, and he wrote what we know as I Corinthians to respond to these problems and questions.

I Corinthians is an amazing letter. It had to be, given the depth and complexity of the issues facing the Corinthian community. No other letter which we have from Paul treats more subjects more profoundly than does this one. To read and study it is to receive a grand overview of Christian theology and morality. Considered in its relatively short sixteen chapters are: the meaning and nature of salvation, the source and bond of Christian community, sexual morality, marriage, idolatry, conscience, apostleship, the role of women in the Church, sacramental theology (especially that of the Eucharist), spiritual gifts, and the Resurrection.

Chapter 7:   Paul's Introduction to His Letter: Competing Groups Within the Church at Corinth

Please read I Corinthians 1:1-16. Paul follows the customary letter-writing etiquette of his time by beginning his letter with an elaborate greeting (1:1-3) and thanksgiving (1:4-9). There are some subtle touches, however, which already reveal his skill as a correspondent. He uses even formalities to his advantage and shrewdly constructs his introduction so that it begins to make many of the points which he will hammer home in the main body of the letter.

Considering that some of the Corinthians had rejected Paul's authority, were acting as if they had transcended Christian morality, and had contented themselves with a narrow understanding of Church, it is striking that Paul manages to assert his authority as an apostle (1:1), issue a call to holiness, and place the Corinthian community in the larger context of the universal Church (1:2)—all within the space of his introductory greeting!

While his thanksgiving is undoubtedly genuine, it is also gently ironic. In contrast to the faith, love, and hope of the Thessalonians (see I Thes 1:3), the only things Paul mentions in regard to the Corinthians are two charismatic gifts (1:5) which, as the rest of the letter will show, are of relatively minor importance.

The introduction witnesses to the Christ-centeredness of this particular letter and of Paul's theology in general. He refers to Christ (or a variation of this name) some nine times in these nine verses. Four times in this short space he calls Jesus "Lord." This term may be a commonplace to us, but in Paul's day it was a title which trembled with power, since it was the word most frequently used for God in the Hebrew Scriptures, as well as a deific designation of the Roman emperor. To "call on the name of our Lord Jesus Christ" (1:2) was equivalent to calling upon the name of Yahweh (see, for example, Psalm 99:6); it also proclaimed the fact that a Christian's first loyalty was to Christ, not to Caesar.

Twice Paul uses his favorite phrase "in Christ" (a phrase occurring some 165 times during the course of his letters). This is one of the most loaded expressions in the entire New Testament, carrying as it does the meaning of a personal relationship with Christ which is so intimate that it empowers one to become like Christ.

As in his letters to the Thessalonians, Paul's first letter to the

Corinthians is saturated in his expectation of the Lord's imminent return. Statements such as "the revelation of our Lord Jesus Christ" (1:7) and "the day of our Lord Jesus" (1:8) refer to the Second Coming.

The last two verses of the introduction (1:8-9) are especially significant theologically. Echoing his major concern in the letter to the Galatians, Paul stresses the fact that it is God's faithfulness in Christ which justifies (enables one to stand "blameless"). The emphasis, in other words, is on God's grace, not human accomplishment.

Paul has learned of the infighting troubling the Corinthian church and appeals for reconciliation. He cites four competing groups, each claiming its own leader, without, however, that leader's consent. Tactfully, he first names the group which claims him as its authority. He was the first Christian missionary to visit Corinth. His style of proclaiming the Gospel appealed largely to the poor and the uneducated. The Pauline faction probably was composed of such people.

After Paul's departure, another missionary, Apollos, visited Corinth. Apollos was from Alexandria, the greatest intellectual center of that time, famed for its allegorical approach to Scripture, which read layer upon layer of not-too-apparent spiritual meanings into the biblical text. Apollos was a master of this method. While his message was sound enough in itself, his esoteric style appealed to those who were already tempted by gnosticism, a philosophic fad of the day which maintained that secret knowledge was the key to heaven.

Another clique claimed Peter (Cephas is its Aramaic form) as its head. These were Jewish Christians who emphasized the continuing importance of the law. There was probably a fourth party, one which boasted direct, charismatic revelations from the Lord.

The picture Paul paints is an embarrassing one, analogous to a typical marketplace scene in which different merchants, with basically the same wares, are vigorously hawking their own merchandise. At this wretched situation he hurls a barrage of pointed questions

(1:13), calculated to shame through sarcasm. Again he uses the image of the name; this time to remind the Corinthians that—just as in their business transactions, purchased goods or services were said to pass ''to the name'' of the new owner—so their common baptism in the name of Christ precludes any competing loyalties.

Questions for Personal Reflection/Group Discussion:

1. What does the phrase ''in Christ Jesus'' mean to you personally?
2. If Paul were to step into your parish church, what competing groups would he see in need of reconciliation with one another?
3. What transcending realities do you think Paul would appeal to for reconciliation?

Chapter 8: **Triple Foolishness:**
Salvation, the Composition of the Corinthian Church,
and Paul's Method of Preaching

Please read I Corinthians 1:17-2:5.   Against this backdrop of disharmony, Paul goes on to describe the situation from a radically different point of view. It is as if we had surveyed the scene from a marketplace perspective and then were suddenly transported to a mountaintop, where the prospect is alarmingly changed. He challenges the worldviews of both the Greeks and the Jews. By thus lumping together the backgrounds of the two major ethnic groups in the church at Corinth, he hopes to encourage each side to see its narrowness, and to transcend this narrowness through a higher vision.

   In contradistinction to the pet theories of the Greeks and the pet theologies of the Jews, Paul describes a strategy of salvation which is supremely God's. The ''wisdom'' mentioned in 1:17 could also be translated as ''philosophy.'' What he is protesting here is the dominant motif of Greek philosophy in relation to God; that is, the fact that

God, to be God, must be distant and must be impersonal. To the cultured Greek who wanted to think his way to God, the Christian realities of the incarnation and the suffering of God were not only metaphysically impossible, but aesthetically revolting. To the Greeks the notion of a God become man to die was "madness" (as the *Jerusalem Bible* translates the "absurdity" of 1:23).

The Jews could not accept the reality of a crucified Messiah because the prevailing tenor of their theology militated against it. In spite of the presence of the theme of redemptive suffering in the prophets, this perspective remained subordinate to the more popular theme of vengeance and retribution. Thus, because most Jews expected a warring Messiah, they were not able to recognize, much less accept, a suffering one. To the Jews the notion of a suffering Messiah was an impossible "stumbling block" (1:23).

The course of events surrounding the life, death, and Resurrection of Jesus proved both Greek theory and Jewish theology to be irreparably off target. The most learned representatives of each culture—the Greek philosopher and the Jewish master of the law (1:20)—were equally mistaken. Each was looking in the wrong place in the wrong way; the Jew expecting obliterating "signs" of supernatural power; the Greek awaiting the "wisdom" of the ultimate argument (1:22).

Paul knew exactly what he was doing when he set up his disputation the way he did: Greek philosophy and Jewish theology on the one hand, the unmitigated reality of the cross on the other. The two major cultural groups in Corinth also represented the two major "religious" alternatives in the world at that time. By exposing both as equally far from the truth of the Gospel, he was in effect, making the shocking point that humankind's best attempts were not only ineffective but misguided. This sets the stage of his forceful summary statement of the Gospel's inversion of human thought and action: "For God's folly is wiser than man, and his weakness more powerful than men" (1:25). This short section (1:17-25) is a celebration of the contradiction of the cross without parallel in the entire New Testament.

Having made his point in terms of universals, Paul proceeds to illustrate it in terms of two particulars, both of them supremely foolish from a human point of view: the makeup of the Corinthian church (1:26-31), and the style of his own preaching (2:1-5).

For the most part, those called to be Church at Corinth are glaringly unsuccessful by the world's standards (1:26). This is just as it should be, for God's ways are not our own. The effect of 1:27-29 is to reduce everyone to the same level of dependency on God. Intelligence, wealth, and family connections are of no advantage when it comes to finding God. Indeed, the pitfall of all three is that they so easily lead to self-sufficiency, and thus eventually to self-destruction. Paul uses a threefold "God chose" in 1:27-28 (the "he singled out" in v. 27b is literally "God chose") to contrast God's initiative with human arrogance. It is God who calls us, not we who claim God.

The "God chose" refrain leads up to the powerful little creed in 1:30, a fine statement of "The Gospel According to Paul." The lead, as always, is the Father's. Through the initiative of the Father, Jesus has become four crucial things for us: 1. Our *wisdom*. This does not mean abstract, intellectual knowledge, but the lifegiving relationship springing from an intimate personal union with the Lord. 2. Our *justice*. The emphasis here, as it is in so much of the Old Testament, is on God's faithfulness to his promises. Nothing that we can do can make us "just" in God's eyes—the only deed that can save us is God's allegiance to his pledge of salvation. 3. Our *sanctification*. Sanctification is both the result and the process of becoming holy. We are already holy because of our relationship with Christ; a deepening response to our relationship with Christ enables us to become progressively "more" holy. 4. Our *redemption*. This summarizes the saving reality of wisdom, justice, and sanctification through Christ. The word comes from the slave market, where "redemption" was the procedure by which a slave could save his or her purchase price and deposit the money (which the slave's master would later claim) in a temple, thereby earning the protection of the resident divinity—and freedom. The process is reversed in the context of Christianity, where it is God who redeems us, not we who redeem ourselves.

Just as the Christian community at Corinth is an outlandish composition according to the rhythm of the world, so too is Paul's method of preaching (2:1-5). Both echo the absurdity of the Gospel, which he has already established in 1:17-25. The bedrock of his preaching is "God's testimony" (2:1).

"Testimony" (*martyrion*) is a legal term referring to evidence so strong as to constitute proof. Significantly, it is the root of our English word "martyr," a person whose death constitutes proof positive of the power of faith. The testimony which Paul is citing in 2:1 is the redemptive death-Resurrection of Christ, God's ultimate confirmation of his saving presence in Jesus. The outrageous reality of this event precludes the use of the kind of glib rhetoric which was so much a part of Greek philosophy at this time. The Christ-event was from God; therefore the motivating power to accept this event came not from the ability of the preacher, or from one's own grasp of the message, but simply from God. To communicate this sense of our underlying dependence on God, Paul mentions the "convincing power of the Spirit" (2:4). While the theological concept of the Trinity had not yet been formulated, this kind of thinking on Paul's part reveals that his understanding of God was already thoroughly trinitarian in substance. He goes on to develop the notion of illumination by the Spirit in the next section of his letter.

Questions for Personal Reflection/Group Discussion:

1. During Paul's time, the Jews demanded "signs" and the Greeks looked for "wisdom." What kinds of "proofs" do many of our contemporaries look for today so that they can "find" God.?
2. If Paul were here today, how do you think he would respond to our contemporary demand for proof?

**Chapter 9:   The Source of Real Wisdom;
The Nature of True Apostleship**

Please read I Corinthians 2:6-4:21.   This portion of the letter continues in the same vein as that which precedes it; the wisdom of the world is still being contrasted with the wisdom of God. Here, however, Paul intensifies his thought and speaks from the context of Christian maturity in the Spirit.

''A certain wisdom which we express among the spiritually mature'' (2:6), does not refer to a type of caste system within Christianity, but to an advance in insight and practice which *all* Christians are challenged to make. Paul assumes that a Christian will progress from infancy to maturity, from being fed with ''milk'' to being given ''solid food'' (3:2); in other words, to advance from the basic facts of the faith to a deeper understanding of how these facts fit together, and how they empower us to greater acts of loving service.

He makes a telling change when he quotes Isaiah 64:3 in 2:9. The concluding words in the original text read ''wait for him.'' He has replaced ''wait for'' with ''love.'' The period of waiting for God is over; he has come to us in the person of Jesus, and now it is possible to love him. Love is a more concrete, tangible reality than hope; hope may patiently wait, but love has the power to transform the whole of one's life. As we shall see from much of the rest of this letter, it is precisely to this type of total transformation—one which involves the body as well as the soul, morality as well as spirituality—that Paul is calling the Corinthians. His use of the word love here hints at the pivotal role love will play later on in the letter, especially in chapter 13.

Paul's vision of the Christian life is not static, but developmental. A Christian is supposed to deepen, to move from the basic facts to their interrelationships and implications. But how does one do this? Apparently some of the Corinthians were beginning to equate growth in the Christian life with philosophical learning; others were seeking Christian maturity in a return to legalism. Against these (and any other) forms of human wisdom, Paul insists that the crucial principle of empowerment is God himself, through the power of his Spirit (3:10).

Since the Spirit is the "Spirit of God" (3:11), it communes with the deepest realities of God. Since the Spirit Christians have received is also "God's Spirit" (3:12), we, too, can commune with God in depth. But there's more. In 3:16b Paul uses the word "mind" as an equivalent to "spirit." The text could be paraphrased as "But we have the Spirit of Christ." Notice how in this short section (3:10-16), God, the Spirit, and Christ are each mentioned, and mentioned in such a way that there is the closest possible communion between them.

Again, the theological term "Trinity" had not yet been born, but these kinds of equations on Paul's part indicate that the Church experienced God in a trinitarian way long before the official declaration. Moreover, because the Spirit we have received is God's (and, by implication, Christ's) we may infer that the Christian, by cooperating with the Spirit, actually shares in the life of the Trinity! As we shall see in chapter 12 of this letter, this type of thinking figures prominently in Paul's image of the mystical body.

The key to real wisdom, according to Paul, is actually quite simple. It is, first of all, to make personal contact with God, the source of real wisdom, by accepting his testimony (2:1)—his Word according to Christ—as true. This first step would include baptism, becoming "consecrated in Christ" (1:2). The second step would be to offer oneself for progressive transformation by God's Spirit (2:10). Negatively, this would involve avoiding the spirit of the world (2:12), the so-called wisdom of the natural man (2:14), a person who, body and soul, is caught up in vain attempts of self-salvation. Positively, the second, or "growth" step for a Christian means cooperating with the presence of the Spirit in one's life, allowing oneself to become a spiritual man (2:15), a person who, body and soul, is caught up in the life of God.

At this point, in 3:1-4, Paul straightforwardly expresses his disappointment in the Corinthians. When he was with them, introduc ing them to the Gospel, he had to concentrate on the basic facts of God's testimony in Christ. He assumed that maturity would follow. It did not. Instead of growth in Christian maturity, dissension followed. This makes Paul question the depth of their initial conversion.

Having reopened the subject of factions, Paul's thought turns to their unwitting leaders. The Corinthians had lost perspective on the meaning of ministry. They were rallying around various Christian leaders as if these men were gospels-unto-themselves, and not merely God's servants. As in the previous parts of the letter, his tactic is to stress God's overriding role in the whole process of transmitting and receiving the Gospel. Different ministers are called to different tasks; none of their activity would amount to anything were it not for the life-giving presence of God within their work.

One of the delightful things about reading St. Paul is his intense use of metaphor. In his passion to communicate, he will pile image upon image or, as in 3:9, one metaphor will trigger the use of another, and he will switch figures in mid thought. Farming suddenly turns into construction, and with this new metaphor his line of thinking goes off on a slightly different trajectory. Instead of the sower, he is now the master-builder who has had only the opportunity to lay the foundation before being called off on another job. The foundation, of course, is the critical item, and he is confident that he has done his task well because the foundation he laid in Jesus Christ is the only sure one (3:10). All additions to the building will be judged against the absolute standard of Christ. His list of glaringly disparate building materials (3:12) betrays the fact that he considers some additions to be much more worthy than others. The introduction of the powerful picture of Judgment Day—complete with its attendant image of trial by fire— underlines the seriousness with which he considers the Christian ministry.

Paul's thought takes another turn and the building image turns into an image of the Christian community at Corinth being the temple of God (3:16-17). This was a radical metaphor, calling forth as it did the whole Jewish tradition of the Temple and the presence of God in its inner sanctuary, the Holy of Holies. What he does by using this daring image is to claim the Christian community as the focal point of God's presence in the world. Later on in this letter (6:19) he will extend this temple metaphor to the individual Christian. We need to remember, however, that its communal dimension is primary.

The image of the temple leads to an implied contrast between the true temple of God, whose foundation is the foolishness of the Gospel, and various types of "unholy" temples, the foundations of which are worldly wisdom and competitiveness (3:18-21b).

Paul concludes this intensely metaphorical section of his letter (3:5-3:21b) by piling image upon image in a wild romp that begins with the names of those whom the Corinthians claim as the leaders of their factions and ends with a vision of the mystical body. This is a compelling call to the Corinthians to give up their factions by placing them in an incredibly bigger perspective.

The prose is definitely soaring, and we seem to be on the verge of getting a glimpse into heaven, when Paul abruptly returns to the topic of true apostleship. He stresses the element of servanthood (4:1a) and places this within the context of stewardship (4:1b, 2). The word translated as "administrator" in the NAB (4:2) is literally "steward," and carries with it some rich connotations.

In the ancient world, a steward was a trusted servant or slave to whom the master gave complete authority for the administration of his estate. Thus, the position of steward simultaneously brought with it total jurisdiction over those things entrusted to it, yet total dependency on the will of the master—a perfect term to describe the role of an apostle. Because of the pivotal nature of this position, an apostle is directly responsible to the Lord; no lesser authority than God is adequate to judge his ministry and motivation.

Paul goes on to state that he has been using himself and Apollos as positive examples to illustrate the nature of true apostleship. He challenges the Corinthians to follow their lead in faithfully handing on the content of the apostolic tradition ("not to go beyond what is set down" 4:6b), and not to get caught up in purely human predilections of style. Preferring the teaching of one apostle to that of another is nothing but conceit; it is simply another form of attempting to earn one's way into heaven, this time through having the proper connections. Not only did each of the factions in the Corinthian church claim its own spiritual guide, it actually took credit for the content of their teacher's teaching. As if to underscore their arrogance, Paul reminds the Corinthians of the priority of God's grace (4:7b), without which they would have and be literally nothing.

At this point he slips into sarcasm to hammer home his message. He charges the Corinthians with self-satisfaction (4:8), fires in the irritating simile of apostles being like captives marching to a brutal death in a Roman triumphal procession (4:9a), and bitterly contrasts the self-sacrificing ways of the apostles with the self-important ways of the Corinthians (4:9b-13).

Then, almost predictably, his manner swings from harsh sarcasm to tender pleading. He calls the Corinthians his "beloved children" (4:14), reminds them of his unique relationship with them as their spiritual father (4:15), and entreats them to follow his example (4:16).

Next, he informs the Corinthians that Timothy, his special representative, is on his way, and that he himself will follow shortly (4:17-19). The purpose of his visit is avowedly a test. The pleasantness or unpleasantness of the visit will depend on their obedience or disobedience to the reforms which Paul, with full authority as an apostle, is asking for in this letter (4:20-21).

Questions for Personal Reflection/Group Discussion:

1. Which aspects of your relationship with God would you describe as "milk"; that is, beginning steps?
2. Which aspects of your relationship with God would you describe as "solid food"; that is, more mature steps or stages in your life as a Christian?
3. What happens to a Christian when he or she never "grows up"?

4. Why is it important to gradually outgrow the totally "milk" stage of one's faith (not that milk shouldn't continue to be an essential part of one's diet!)?
5. How is 3:6 ("I planted the seed and Apollos watered it, but God made it grow") a vitally important call to perspective for any Christian leader?
6. What are some of the metaphors you most often use in describing your faith to others?
7. Do you think that Paul's blunt expression of feelings helps or hinders him in communicating the Gospel? Why?

Chapter 10:   Responses to a Number of Moral Issues, Including Sex

Please read I Corinthians 5:1-6:20.   Paul has learned, quite possibly from the same source that informed him about the factions (see I Cor 1:11), that the Corinthian church has blatantly disregarded the case of a man being in a sexual relationship with his stepmother. Such conduct was considered scandalous by both Jews and Greeks, although certain rabbis did permit exceptions. Paul does not hesitate to use his apostolic authority to correct the situation (5:3-5); his sure sense of his own power to judge this matter seems to point to the fact that Jesus really did give special authority to his apostles; perhaps it hints at Jesus' words in John 20:23: "If you forgive men's sins, they are forgiven them; if you hold them bound, they are held bound."

The course of action which he mentions in 5:2, "getting rid of the offender," and his exhortation in 5:3 to "expel the wicked man from your midst," suggest that the punishment he had in mind was that of excommunication. This practice had its precedent in the Old Testament, where serious offenders were sometimes expelled from the body of the people. Paul reflects an understanding of the importance of community which is similar to that of the Hebrew Scriptures: one is saved, not as an individual, but through belonging to God's people. To be cut off from one's people meant nothing less than to lose one's life-giving relationship with God. Thus, excommunication was seen as the ultimate punishment. It should be noted, however, that excommunication was rarely permanent; it was seen as the vehicle of last resort to effect a sinner's reformation and eventual reentry into the Church.

The only acceptable form of boasting for Paul is "boasting in the Lord"; that is, celebrating all that the *Lord* has been able to accomplish through one's ministry. The Corinthians, on the other hand, have apparently been boasting about their own accomplishments, taking personal credit for what God has been able to work in them. Paul links his censure to a warning (5:6). He uses the yeast-dough metaphor in a negative way to point out the probable outcome of their self-satisfaction unless it is checked: they will be ruined, just as yeast "ruins" dough.

Paul's reference to unleavened bread (5:7a) reminds him of its ritual significance at Passover which triggers, in turn, a connection between Christ and Passover (5:7b). The sacrificial nature of the Passover lamb prefigures Jesus' sacrifice at Calvary. Although Paul does not specifically mention the Eucharist here, given his rather lengthy discussion of it later on in this letter (10:14-22; 11:17-34), it seems likely that the Passover meal, both for him and for his readers, had eucharistic connotations. It also seems probable that these connotations were along the line of sacrifice, since this was one of the main themes of Passover.

In 5:9-13 Paul responds to a misunderstanding occasioned by a previous letter. Unless, as some scholars think, we have this document wholly or partially in II Corinthians 6:14-7:1 (which fits the description in 5:9 admirably well), this earlier letter has been lost, and suggests the likely possibility of other lost letters. At any rate, the Corinthians had taken Paul's injunction not to associate with immoral persons out of its proper context, and had consequently put themselves into an impasse. By applying his mandate to the world at large, it became difficult, if not impossible, to live in the world. He acknowledges this when he says "To avoid them, you would have to leave the world!" (5:10b). Paul goes on to clarify that what he wrote about avoiding immoral persons was intended for the discipline and well-being of the Church. Actually, the verdict of excommunication which he just gave (5:2-5) is a specific instance of the basic principle of avoiding serious sinners.

Again, given Paul's extensive treatment of the meal aspect of the Eucharist, it seems likely that his command not to eat with the seriously sinful (5:11b) includes not eating the Lord's Supper with them.

Paul's next major complaint is against Christians who go to law with one another before civil courts (6:1-8). He begins his argument by alluding to a strand of late Jewish apocalyptic tradition whichasserts that when the Messiah comes, his loyal followers will exercise judgment with him over both men and angels. Given this promise, he is incredulous that Christians should go to unbelievers for justice. This reminder of future glory leads up to his more substantive criticism in 6:7, which is the fact that they bring lawsuits against one another at all. Such conduct is in glaring violation of Christ's example.

Not content to confront merely those who are into lawsuits, Paul goes on to challenge those who are apparently into quite a number of other things as well (6:9-11). One gets the impression that there has been quite a lot of backsliding in the church at Corinth. To counter this backsliding, he issues a warning and a reminder. The warning is to the effect that it is possible to lose one's salvation by rejecting one's relationship with Christ and returning to one's pre-Christian ways. The reminder is to the powerful reality of their salvation. It is as if he is asking the Corinthians to remember their conversion, and in the process of remembering to reaffirm the promises they made and the new life they received at baptism. Note the quasi-trinitarian formula he uses in 6:11, perhaps indicative that the Church already was baptising in the name of the Father, Son, and Holy Spirit.

The most common form of immorality in the city of Corinth was sexual promiscuity. Undoubtedly this was one of the most common shortcomings within the Christian community at Corinth as well. In the next section of his letter (6:12-20), Paul goes to considerable length to point out the seriousness of this sin. He does not merely insist on the grave sinfulness of sexual relations outside of the marriage relationship, but explains *why* such actions are seriously sinful. This explanation is his earliest description of what has since come to be called the doctrine of the "Mystical Body of Christ." The pattern of relationship pictured here is fundamental to both an adequate understanding of theology and an adequate practice of Christian morality.

Paul begins his discussion by using a popular Greek form of argumentation, the diatribe (6:12-13). This was a sophistic form of debate in which one would wear out one's opponents by clever critiques of their major philosophical positions. Paul's opponents here are certain libertines within the Corinthian church who have picked up his own maxim "Everything is lawful for me" and turned it to their own advantage; that is, used it to support their own penchant for sexual variety. These libertines were sharp enough to have known that the backbone of Paul's theology is relationship with Christ, and that true freedom flows *from* this relationship, not counter to it. Thus, his maxim contained a built-in safeguard, the requirement of acting "in" the Lord. It was similar to Augustine's saying "Love God and do what you will" several centuries later; it being assumed that if one really loved God he wouldn't do just anything, but only those things which were pleasing to God.

The libertines, then, had pounced on Paul's maxim and turned it into a battle cry for sexual license. They had turned a statement which he intended as an expression of Christian freedom into a new slogan for an old form of slavery—slavery to sex. In addition to St. Paul, the libertines were quoting from the popular philosophy of the day, a philosophy which held not only that "Food is for the stomach and the stomach for food," but also the derivative postulate that just as it is necessary and good to satisfy one's appetite for food, so also it is necessary and good to satisfy one's appetite for sex. As we can see from the substance of his argument, Paul is not so concerned to exonerate his pet phrase as he is to combat this fallacious line of reasoning. Abusing his maxim was a relatively minor matter; the ethos of Greek philosophy, however, was a matter of serious concern, since it had already made such foreboding inroads into the practice of Christian morality in Corinth.

The Greek attitude toward the body was one of deprecation. The soul was thought to be imprisoned within the body. Immortality was the soul's final escape from bodily limitations. This pervasively negative attitude toward the body expressed itself in two extremes of behavior. On the one hand, the degradation of the body could lead to a stringent asceticism. This was the rigorous alternative, one not very popular in Greek society as a whole. On the other hand, maintaining that the body had no intrinsic value could also lead to the view that nothing that one did with one's body really mattered. This was the lax, and popular, alternative. It opened the door to sexual promiscuity and/or the practice of homosexuality. Such was the philosophical position of the libertines, a position which Paul insists is incompatible with real Christianity.

Paul gives his main objection to sexual immorality in his third rebuttal of the libertines (6:13b-20). His argument hinges on a combination of Hebrew anthropology and Christian belief in the Resurrection. Significantly, the reality of the Resurrection establishes the validity of the Hebrew understanding of the nature of the human person. As we have seen, the notion of bodily resurrection was offensive to the Greek because he could not conceive of something as base as the body being raised to eternal glory. To the Hebrew, the human person was an indivisible unity of body and soul. When the notion of an afterlife developed in Jewish theology, it was conceived in terms of the same union of body and soul which had characterized earthly existence. Paul was convinced that the bodily Resurrection of Jesus was God's guarantee that a similar resurrection awaited all Christians (6:14).

Paul's unshakable hope in the Resurrection lay in his understanding of mystical union with Christ. In virtue of baptism—which was conceived of as dying to one's old self to be reborn in Christ (see Romans 6:1-11), and presupposed conversion—the Christian entered into a relationship with Christ which was so close that the only credible human analogy would be marriage. Without losing his identity as an individual, the Christian becomes part of Christ, and Christ part of him. Thus, Jesus' life becomes our life, Jesus' Resurrection the promise of our own resurrection.

Given the reality of this intimate relationship with Jesus—a relationship which includes the whole of one's being, including one's bodily existence—it becomes unthinkable to give one's body to another person in a casual sexual union. To do so is, in effect, to leave Christ for someone else. Strictly speaking, to sin in this way is to commit spiritual adultery. It is, as Paul says (6:18), to sin against one's own body (as well as against the other person and against God) because a Christian, in offering his body to a person outside marriage, is breaking his prior commitment to the Lord, a commitment which includes his body.

Paul seals his argument by focusing his image of the temple, which he applies to the Christian community in 3:16, on the individual Christian (6:19). God's presence is not just something "out there." Through the power of the Holy Spirit it is a saving presence—a saving relationship—within each Christian. Paul reminds the Corinthians that they are not their own masters (6:19b). They are like slaves who, because of the incredible price of Calvary, no longer belong to the world, but to God.

This chapter bears the title "Responses to a Number of Moral Issues" and concerns itself with some basic principles of Christian morality. It seems fitting to close our discussion by considering in what sense Paul's teaching *is* basic, or normative, for Christianity. In recent years there has been considerable pressure to make parts of Paul's teaching relative by claiming that they are contingent on the culture of his day; in other words, those parts of his message that are culturally determined can be discarded. Even in certain Christian circles, merely to mention that such-and-such a teaching is culturally determined is enough to discredit it. This kind of thinking can be especially effective in getting certain behavioral expectations, such as chastity, branded as "old-fashioned" or "outdated," and therefore no longer applying to life today.

The texts we have been discussing in this chapter are among the favorite hunting-grounds for cultural determinists. Excommunication is an embarrassment, so it is claimed that this is simply a leftover from the Old Testament which has found its way into Paul's theology. The problem is that Paul is terribly at ease with his authority to enforce this kind of discipline. Presumably he received his authority from somewhere, or rather Someone. The logical conclusion is that Paul got his authority from Christ; this seems likely, particularly given the fact that all four Gospels portray Jesus as quite willing to share his authority with his apostles.

Granted, for the sake of argument, that Paul did indeed receive authorization from Christ, the cultural determinist will reply "But Jesus himself was culturally determined." This point seems to be a major difficulty, because if we take the Incarnation and the humanity of Christ seriously, there *is* a sense in which Jesus has been determined by his culture. After all, he voluntarily limited himself to be a certain person living during a certain time at a certain place, with all the limitations which these conditions imply.

The "problem" of Jesus' true humanity is our only way out. To take the Incarnation seriously is to say nothing less than that God chose to speak to us most fully in and through the fully human limitations of his Son. It means that the full force of God's revelation has become focused in the person of Jesus and that therefore everything this person says and does—culturally conditioned as it may be—becomes a vehicle of contact and communication between God and people. Jesus' understanding of authority was, indeed, Jewish. But its Jewishness is nothing less than the medium through which God chose to communicate his message.

Because God chose to concretize himself in a person, everything this person does becomes super-charged with the power of revelation.

In short, everything Jesus touches becomes transformed: water becomes wine, illness becomes health, Passover becomes Eucharist, death becomes Resurrection.

To return to our original concern, the authority to excommunicate becomes, in Jesus, a means not of punishment (as it had been for the Hebrews), but a means to repentance and return. This is the transformed understanding of the discipline of excommunication which Paul has received and which he, in turn, hands on. What Paul is saying is *not* culturally or historically determined because the Source of its transforming power is beyond culture and beyond history.

But what about the danger of fossilization; that is, the tendency to make one particular expression of a saving reality unchangeable for all time? The Holy Spirit, as the living presence of Christ within the Christian community, inspires and enables that community to come up with new forms to express the old truths. For example, consider the Sacrament of Reconciliation. We know that reconciliation-healing was a vital part of Jesus' ministry, and that he wanted to share his power to heal and to reconcile with the community of his disciples. Unlike the Sacrament of the Lord's Supper, Jesus did not institute a set form for the celebration of reconciliation. Rather, he simply shared this gift with his disciples, and left it up to them (and the presence of the Holy Spirit within them) to decide how best to share this gift with others. Thus, the ministry of healing and reconciliation has been exercised in significantly different ways throughout the history of the Church; all of these ways, however, through the inspiration of the Holy Spirit, have their roots in the historical ministry of Jesus.

Now, let's turn to the subject of sexual morality. Again, those who hold to cultural determinism argue that Paul's thought simply mirrors the prejudices of his Jewish background: Jewish tradition couldn't condone the homosexual act, neither did Paul; Jewish tradition couldn't tolerate genital sex outside of marriage, neither did Paul. According to the cultural determinists, Paul was merely reflecting the limitations of his own culture, limitations which our culture has presumably overcome. Admittedly, this is one possible interpretation of the matter, an interpretation which quite a few of today's Christians are willing to accept because sexual purity, for one reason or another, is distasteful to them.

Another possible interpretation, however, is that Paul's insights spring from revelatory experience as well as culture; that revelation transforms culture in the same way that grace transforms nature. According to this point of view, the reason that Paul cannot countenance premarital or extramarital sexual intercourse is that he has found his own relationship with Christ to be so intimate and so real that the only sexual relationship which comes anywhere near to being analogous is marriage. In other words, marriage is the only relationship in which genital sexuality can begin to reflect the deeper reality of our spiritual marriage with Christ.

For a Christian anything less is a serious distortion of God's relationship with us, echoing casualness instead of commitment, infidelity instead of fidelity, selfishness instead of love. Considered from Paul's perspective, then, sexual promiscuity for the Christian isn't simply a violation of some cultural norm, but an offense against the nature of reality, reality being God's design and not our own invention. From this point of view, what he has to say about sex is not only a basic principle of Christian morality, but a revelatory insight into the real nature of bodily existence.

Questions for Personal Reflection/Group Discussion:

1. What does Paul's image of the Body of Christ reveal to you about the nature of our relationship with God?
2. Why and how do Paul's teachings continue to provide the Church with some basic principles of Christian morality?
3. Summarize Paul's teaching on sexual morality.

Chapter 11: How to Live as a Christian in a Pagan World I: Responses to Questions Pertaining to Marriage

Please read I Corinthians 7. The next four chapters of Paul's letter revolve around two major areas of concern about which the Corinthian church had written Paul for advice: questions centering on marriage and its alternatives, and the question of what to do (To eat or not to eat?) with meat that had been previously offered to idols.

Chapter seven, a series of guidelines on marriage and the single life, contrasts sharply with the last part of chapter six (12-20). There, Paul had been challenging a "liberal" circle within the Christian community—those whose understanding of morality didn't go far enough. Here, in chapter seven, he is addressing "conservative" members of the Church—those whose understanding of morality tended to go too far. Apparently some of these people were saying that all marriages should be dissolved or that, at the least, there should be no more sexual intercourse.

Christians of this persuasion were a little too close to the ascetic (bodily denial) extreme of the libertine-ascetic dichotomy. Given this as his immediate context, what Paul has to say about marriage in this chapter isn't as negative as it might at first appear. He certainly takes exception to their rule of total abstinence for all Christians! As we read this chapter we need to remember that the stimulus for his statements on marriage was a series of questions from the ascetic wing of the Church at Corinth; his response, then, is not a seriously conceived theology, but a string of answers responding to a string of questions.

Another important fact to keep in mind while reading this chapter is that Paul's counsel on this particular matter springs directly from his expectation that Christ would return very soon, certainly within his lifetime. And not just he, but all Christians at this time lived in anticipation of the Second Coming. As it became more and more apparent that Jesus was not coming back as soon as had been expected, the Christian community and its leaders, including St. Paul, were forced to acknowledge the reality of this "new" situation—the prospect of an indefinite, and perhaps lengthy, period of time before the Lord's return. Seen from this perspective, marriage came to take on deeper significance. This enhanced significance was reflected in Paul's later letters, especially in his letter to the Ephesians.

There is a notable difference between what we find in this chapter (I Cor 7), and the understanding of marriage expressed in Ephesians 5. The difference does not lie in one chapter contradicting the other, but in a radical change of perspective. Because time is so foreshortened in Corinthians, its treatment of marriage is severely truncated. Time has opened up by the time Paul was writing Ephesians; its understanding of marriage is expansive and solid. The difference is one of development: his thought has matured from an early rough sketch to a later, more refined canvas.

Paul begins by responding to those who take the hard-line position that marriage shouldn't even be an option for Christians (7:1-2). He cites their basic position that "A man is better off having no relations with a woman," and does not deny it; he will not, however, posit it as a basic principle of Christian living. Rather, he immediately takes exception to it, even if only for the sake of avoiding immorality.

Next (7:3-7), he replies to those who maintain that even if marriage is allowed, sexual intercourse shouldn't be. Again, Paul will not allow this as a basic precept, even though he would prefer personally that all live singly, as he does. He sees the sexual act as an indispensable part of the marriage relationship (7:3), something from which (by a shared decision) partners may abstain for a short time as a spiritual discipline similar to fasting (7:5), but also something which each partner is equally obliged to give the other (7:4). A wife is *not* a sexual object for her husband according to St. Paul!

Paul's next advice is to those who are not married, be they single or widowed (7:8-9). Once more, he counsels singleness as preferable to marriage with the proviso, of course, that marriage is preferable to sexual immorality. To those already married (7:10-11), he does not propose separation, but insists that they fulfill their marriage commitment. In doing so he is faithfully following Jesus' example.

His subsequent instructions (7:12-16) concern mixed marriages, those in which one of the members is a Christian, the other not. These marriages were especially loathsome to the rigorists. Smashing their hopes that such unions would be summarily dissolved, Paul staunchly maintains not only that the Christian has no right to leave his or her non-Christian spouse, but that the unbelieving partner has been purified through the union, making the children legitimate. Paul's great hope for mixed marriages is that the nonbelieving partner may eventually become a Christian. He, of course, cannot legislate for non-Christians; they are free to leave if they so desire. It is interesting to note, in passing, that he introduces these principles by candidly acknowledging that he is not aware that Jesus has left any pronouncements on these matters; nevertheless, he certainly does not hesitate to do so himself. Here is another clear indication of his very real authority as an apostle.

The general principle enunciated in 7:17 ("each one should lead the life the Lord has assigned him, continuing as he was when the Lord called him.") presupposes that the time before Jesus' return is short indeed. It assumes adult converts who are to remain content with their position in life for the brief period before the Second Coming. The inescapable fact that this principle, if taken literally over a long period of time, becomes totally unworkable, suggests an even more basic principle underlying it. Paul hints at this more fundamental principle in 7:19b when he says "What matters is keeping God's commandments," and in 7:23b where he states "Do not enslave yourselves to men." The underlying precept, then, would run something as follows: "Our relationship with God is what counts, and this relationship has no prerequisites. Don't let anything block or compete with this relationship."

Paul returns to his list of marriage questions in 7:25-28, this time dealing with the preferable course of action for virgins. He repeats the advice he gave he gave in 7:8-9—on the one hand, it is better not to marry; on the other hand, it is permissible to do so. The "present time of stress'' which Paul mentions in 7:26 is a reference to the period of time immediately preceding the Second Coming, which he believed was *his* time.

The general principle reappears in 7:29-35, expressed this time in a series of paradoxes (7:29-31), then in some personal observations on the married state (7:32-35). The paradoxes begin and end with allusions to the Parousia, or Second Coming: ''the time is short'' (7:29) and ''the world as we know it is passing away'' (7:31). The cumulative effect of the paradoxes is to point beyond the general rule stated in 7:17 to the more fundamental principle already discussed in that context. In other words, what Paul teaches is not so much a rule of conduct (as we find in 7:17), as it is a basic attitude of detachment regarding the things of this world. The detachment which he is counseling here is not indifference; it is the ability to put everything in its proper perspective by putting God first in our lives.

Paul goes on to share some personal concerns regarding marriage (7:32-35). These concerns reflect the fundamental principle of detachment from worldly goods and wordly relationships expressed in 7:29-31; he is afraid that marriage causes divided loyalty between one's spouse and God. At this stage in his theological development, he sees marriage as more of a hindrance than a help on one's spiritual journey. To be sure, it is the only relationship within which sexual intercourse is at all compatible with one's relationship with God (as we have seen from our discussion of his notion of the Body of Christ in 6:13b-20). It was not until his letter to the Ephesians, however, that he composed a theology of marriage which was truly positive.

Two situations are possible for the context of the next section, 7:36-38. The text could be referring either to the case of a father and his unmarried daughter, or to the circumstance of an engaged couple who are wondering if they should go ahead and get married, given the shortness of time before Jesus' return. Once again Paul tolerates marriage but suggests virginal singleness as the superior alternative.

Paul's final piece of marital counsel pertains to widows (7:39-40). Not to remarry would be the higher choice. A widow can, however, marry again, provided that her husband is a Christian.

Questionfor Personal Reflection/Group Discussion:

1. It is easy to have a superficially negative reaction to chapter 7 if its context is not kept in proper perspective. What is the real issue that Paul is getting at in this chapter, the issue underlying his specific advice on marriage?

Chapter 12: How to Live as a Christian in a Pagan World II: The Dilemma of Idol-Meat

Please read I Corinthians 8. The whole of chapters 8:1-11:1 constitutes a section on the appropriate Christian response to meat which has been sacrificed to idols. In a style similar to his answers to the multitude of marriage concerns covered in chapter 7, Paul begins by responding to a series of questions revolving around this central topic. The subject of whether or not a Christian could eat sacrificial meat seems strangely remote to us today. During Paul's time, however, and especially in a Gentile environment, such as Greece, this was an issue of real concern.

All Christians living in such a culture were faced with the question because most of the meat sold in the public markets had already been offered to pagan deities. The sacrificial practice of the time involved only a token amount of meat actually being burned in honor of the deity. A good share went to the priests for their support. The rest was returned to the person or public institution making the sacrifice. An individual would often throw a dinner party with his part of the meat; this banquet might be held either in the temple of the deity to whom the animal had been sacrificed, or in the individual's private residence. Public officials would sell their portions to the local butchers who, in turn, would sell it in their shops.

Thus, a Christian was faced with this problem at every meal which involved meat. The questions the Corinthians had asked Paul reflected the different contexts in which meat could be eaten: Was it fitting for a Christian to (a) participate in a banquet held at a pagan temple; (b) in a dinner party at a pagan friend's home? Furthermore, what about the propriety of buying meat from the neighborhood meat market? Obviously these questions do not concern Christians today. Yet the way in which Paul responds to these questions and the basic principle he develops for dealing with such issues is as indispensable for today's Christians as it was for Christians of his time.

The factionalism of the Corinthian church expressed itself in two strikingly different approaches to this problem. There was a group which prided itself on its superior knowledge, and which used this knowledge to argue that it was all right for a Christian to eat meat which had been sacrificed to idols, since the gods behind the idols obviously were not real. Another group, probably containing both recent converts from paganism and those of a conservative Jewish Christian persuasion, were not at all comfortable with eating such meat. This practice was much too recent a part of the pagan past of the Gentile members of this group, and inherently offensive to Christians from a strict Jewish background. The actions of the one group were scandalous to those in the other.

Paul begins his response by quoting what was apparently a favorite slogan of the "liberal," meat-eating group. The "know" in 8:1b of the NAB translation is really part of this slogan, translated in the *Revised Standard Version* as "All of us possess knowledge," and in the *Jerusalem Bible* as "We all have knowledge." The slogan served to put down the conservatives (since *all* of us Christians have received knowledge, where's yours?) and to puff up the liberals (we, at least, are enlightened enough not to get hung up on externals).

Paul cannot abide the pompous, self-righteous attitude mirrored in this slogan and immediately takes it on by contrasting knowledge with love (8:1c). His trenchant insight that 'knowledge' inflates, love upbuilds,'' hints at this masterful consideration of love which will come in chapter 13. The word used for love here is the English translation of the Greek *agapé*, which in profane Greek meant simply affectionate gratitude, but which in Christianity becomes the primary term for God's unconditional love.

Verse 2 reminds us of Socrates' contention that the only person possessing wisdom is the one aware of his ignorance, and shows that Paul is conversant with Greek philosophy. His allusion to Socrates is ironic, given the fact that it was the sophisticated Greek faction which claimed this superior knowledge. Verse 3, too, comes as a surprise. One would expect it to read "But if anyone loves God, that man knows God," but Paul puts us in the passive and writes, "that man is known by him." This unusual usage reflects the Christian understanding of *agapé*, where love is, first of all, something which God gives, and we receive. His emphasis on passivity here is itself a subtle criticism of the meat-eating faction. Between the lines he seems to be saying that their approach is too aggressive, too focused on their own actions; in short, too self-centered.

It is obvious by now that Paul is highly critical of the "knowledgeable," indulgent group. He hastens to make clear, however, that he does not dispute their reasoning (8:4b-5); they are right in denying the existence of the beings behind the idols. Christians know that there is only one God who is simultaneously creator and sustainer; they are aware of the close relationship between God the Father, and Jesus Christ, through whom we come to the Father (8:6). It is noteworthy in v.6 that he assumes the pre-existence of Christ, an assumption which points to the early acceptance of this doctrine among the Christian community.

Paul describes the precarious situation of some Gentile converts, persons who just recently were worshipping idols themselves, and who still had a difficult time separating the facts of Christianity from the fictions of pagan religion (8:7). To these new converts, the attitude and actions of their "knowledgeable" Christian brothers and sisters were not only a temptation but a stumbling block. In effect, these "strong" Christians were inducing their weaker brethren to sin.

Paul says bluntly in 8:11-12 that such conduct is not only sinning against the community, but sinning against Christ himself (the implied connection being that of the Mystical Body—that Christ really is present within his community). This follows from the general principle stated in 8:9—"Take care, however, lest in exercising your right you become an occasion of sin to the weak." Although developed in response to a particular situation which no longer applies, this general statement is one of those fundamental principles of Christian morality which stands for all time.

What Paul has done in this chapter is to contrast the response of knowledge with the response of love. The attitudes and actions flowing from knowledge are shown to be limiting, self-important, and hurting. Those flowing from love are shown to be freeing, self-sacrificing, and healing. Seen from this perspective, Paul's insights in chapter 8 are as challenging to Christian living in the twentieth century as they were for Christians living in the first. Now, as well as then, his words hold the key to reconciliation, the only solid foundation for renewal.

Questions for Personal Reflection/Group Discussion:

1. What is the general moral principle underlying Paul's advice on the eating of idol-meat?
2. Do you think that this is a principle which Catholics today adequately follow? Why or why not?

Chapter 13:   How to Live as a Christian in a Pagan World III: The Seriousness of the Faith

Please read I Corinthians 9.   Like Jesus, Paul became particularly vehement when faced with any form of self-righteousness. The attitude and actions of the "knowledgeable," self-sufficient, meat-eating minority were such a serious distortion of the Gospel that he challenges this faction at length. Chapter 9 continues the confrontation between him and this elitist circle within the Corinthian church.

Paul offers himself as a model of one who has followed the moral principle outlined in 8:9, 13. He begins by citing his own personal freedom (he does not consider himself bound by idols any more than the meat-eaters do), his considerable authority as an apostle (with the implication that those who carry greater duties enjoy greater privileges), his firsthand encounter of the Lord during his conversion experience, and the obvious confirmation of his apostolic work through the existence of a flourishing Christian community in Corinth (9:1-2).

There were those within this community who questioned Paul's claim to be an apostle. Some of his strongest opposition came from this "know-it-all" faction, which asserted that it had greater knowledge than Paul, and that therefore it was not bound by his authority. One of their favorite arguments, or "proofs" that he was not really the apostle he claimed to be was the fact that he would not accept payment for his services, but insisted on providing for himself through his income as a tentmaker. They probably had a catchphrase to the effect that the greater the teaching the more it was worth; since Paul charged nothing, it followed that his teaching was worth nothing.

In defense of his ministry, Paul delivers a list of apostolic privileges (9:3-14), rights to which he, like all the other apostles, is entitled. Among these privileges are freedom from Jewish dietary regulations and freedom to eat meat which has been sacrificed to idols (9:4), the option to marry (9:5), and the right to an income from one's apostolic work (9:6a). Paul greatly expands this last one—the prerogative of earning an income from proclaiming the Good News—because this is the point which has hit him hardest personally.

He lists several other job-related situations which he considers to be similar to apostolic work in the sense that the employee is entitled to his living from them: the soldier, the farmer, and the shepherd (9:6b-7). Then, to further substantiate his argument, he cites an example from the Old Testament which he believes establishes a precedent for the justness of being paid for apostolic work (9:8-10). The example he uses (Deut 25:4) states that an ox shall be allowed to eat of the grain that it is grinding. He employs this case in a typological way (that is, he sees in this O.T. text a foreshadowing of a deeper Christian reality) to prove his point that an apostle, too, must be allowed to eat as just compensation for his labor.

Paul then indulges in one of his favorite techniques in speaking and writing: the rhetorical question (9:11-12a). It should be obvious that if the right to a living is the privilege of an apostle, he can claim this right to a unique degree from the church at Corinth, since he founded it and is its spiritual father.

It looks as if Paul has gone to such great length to make his point precisely so that his own example will stand out all the more. "But we have not used this right. On the contrary, we put up with all sorts of hardships so as not to place any obstacle in the way of the gospel of Christ" (9:12b). Remembering the larger context of his criticism of those who have turned their freedom to eat idol-meat into a stumbling block for weaker Christians, we can see that he positively views his refusal to accept payment for his work as analogous to what these "strong" Christians *should* be doing: that is, freely giving up one of their rights for the good of the greater community. He throws out another rhetorical question (9:13) before clinching his point by referring to one of Jesus' teachings in 9:14.

Paul's refusal to accept payment for his preaching was one of the most controversial aspects of his apostleship. Given the fact that such payment was not only recognized by the Church, but was also part of the social etiquette of the time, his refusal attracted attention. Furthermore, his insistence on pulling his own purse strings was a slap in the face to those who would have liked to exert their influence on him through financial pressures. He is fiercely proud of his independence (9:15), yet admits that this is certainly not the basis of his vocation. Rather, he sees his ministry squarely within the context of prophetic calling.

Paul's words in 9:16b, "I am under compulsion and have no choice. I am ruined if I do not preach it!" remind us of the prophet Jeremiah's words (Jer 20:9)—"I say to myself, I will not mention him, I will speak in his name no more. But then it becomes like fire burning in my heart, imprisoned in my bones; I grow weary holding it in, I cannot endure it." Because he sees himself so clearly as God's voice, he views his work as part of a divine call, not as a normal human vocation. He is under orders to share the Good News. The News is God's, not his. To accept payment for it would be incommensurate with the nature of the Giver. Paul claims payment enough in being able to offer the Gospel as freely as God gave it to him (9:18).

Still expanding on the general principle embedded in 8:13, Paul continues to draw examples from his own ministry, this time to illustrate how adaptable he has been to the needs of others. Written between the lines here is the implication that if *he* can be so gracious, why can't the "knowledgeable" express similar tact in their dealings with those offended by the eating of idol-meat? He mentions three specific instances where he has demonstrated his adaptability: in his ministry to the Jews (9:20), the Gentiles (9:21), and to the "weak" (9:22). This naming of the "weak" is a direct challenge to the "knowledgeable," since it is precisely these "weak" whom the "knowledgeable" are offending.

Paul's parenthetical statements in 9:20c and 9:21b are significant because they define the limits of his adaptability. He is not advocating that a Christian be anything for anybody. What he is saying is that in non-essential matters—such as the observance of Jewish dietary regulations—it is fitting for a Christian to bend, not only so as not to give offense, but as a positive gesture of reaching out to others. Paul takes it for granted that Christians will not go around adapting essentials—anything pertaining to the "law of Christ," which covers the fundamentals of faith and morals.

Paul was quite skillful in using imagery that could really speak to his audience. Jesus chose his metaphors to correspond with the way of life of the people with whom he was communicating; thus he used primarily agricultural imagery. Paul was from a large city and ministered to people in urban centers; his metaphors reflect the multicolored life of the typical Roman metropolis of the middle of the first century.

In addition to its fame as a transportation center and its notoriety for loose living, Corinth was noted for its Isthmian Games, athletic competitions held every two years, and second only to the Olympic Games as the major sporting event of Greece. Paul now makes use of imagery from these games (9:24-25). Speaking still to the faction which considered itself "knowledgeable," he hopes that his description of the deadly seriousness of athletic competition will encourage them to take their Christianity more seriously. His observation that "Athletes deny themselves all sorts of things" (9:25) is a strong hint that it might be a good idea if the "knowledgeable" began denying themselves a few things too, like meat which was an offense to their weaker brethren.

Paul goes on to apply his athletic metaphor to himself (9:26-27). He remarks on the seriousness of his own faith and ministry and concludes with the curious statement "for fear that after having preached to others I myself should be rejected" (9:27b). This little phrase is significant on two counts. First, in speaking from the viewpoint of the human response to God's grace, he acknowledges that it is possible for a person to lose salvation, not through an arbitrary decision on God's part, but from personal carelessness and lack of resolution. In this context 9:26-27 constitutes a stern warning against Christian self-complacency. This is a kind of counterbalance to Paul's overwhelming emphasis on God's grace. Grace is, indeed, primary, but the quality of our response to God is also to be taken into account.

Secondly, from an autobiographical point of view, this text reveals that Paul did not presume his own salvation. This is simply his way of saying that the final word must be God's not ours. His relationship with Christ is far too close for him to overstep his position and take the lead. For there to be a real relationship between God and man, God must be God, and man must be man. In other words, a constituent part of our friendship with God must be the humble acknowledgment that God is the one who does the saving and that we are the ones who are saved. Paul knew this reality well, and consistently refused to claim something which only God can give.

Admittedly, there is a theological tension here between faith and works. This, after all, is to be expected, if theology is in some sense a reflection of reality, and reality with God is relationship. The tension here is precisely the same tension that is found in all love relationship worthy of the name. It is the creative tension between being in love (which is analogous to faith) and expressing that love to the beloved (which is analogous to works). In an intimate relationship of this kind, it is only natural to ask oneself if one's expressions of love are adequate or acceptable. Seen from this perspective Paul's comment about being fearful in 9:27 is not so much a sign of doubt as it is a powerful testimony to the depth and the passion of his relationship with God.

Questions for Personal Reflection/Group Discussion:

1. In what sense is Christianity a supremely serious religion?
2. How might the seeming contradiction "We both *can* and *can't* be sure of our salvation" make good relational sense?

Chapter 14:   How to Live as a Christian in a Pagan World IV: Sacrifice and Salvation

Please read I Corinthians 10:1-11:1   Still speaking from within the framework of the seriousness of the Christian calling, Paul expands his discussion by making several significant references to the Old Testament (10:1-13). Although this portion of the letter continues to be addressed most directly to the "knowledgeable," Christians with a Gentile, and Greek, background (who presumably have received enough catechetical instruction prior to their baptismal conversion to be able to make sense of the Old Testament), the content of this section will be of special interest to Christians with a Jewish background.

Paul approaches the Old Testament typologically; that is, he sees the events described therein as prefigurations of New Testament realities. Thus, "under the cloud" and "through the sea" (10:1-2)—two significant parts of the Exodus experience—become foreshadowings of Christian Baptism. Similarly, the "spiritual food" and "spiritual drink" which the Israelites received in the desert (10:3-4a), point to the Eucharist. His comment in 10:4b about the spiritual rock goes back to a popular rabbinic legend which told of the rock which Moses struck for water following the people around so that they would always have a fresh supply. Paul uses even this legend as a typological pointer to Christ!

The main point, however, comes in 10:5, where Paul bluntly states that in spite of these incredible blessings, most of the people who participated in these events were not saved. The unmistakable implication is that just as many of the Hebrews did not gain salvation through their proto-sacraments, so also Christians will not be saved merely by going through the motions of Baptism and Eucharist.

Continuing to use Old Testament types as forceful examples for the Christian factions in Corinth, Paul goes on to tell the Corinthians *why* so many of the Hebrews failed to attain salvation, in spite of the fact that God was so manifestly present with them. They failed because they turned to idolatry (10:7), gave in to sexual immorality (10:8), refused to trust in the Lord, (10:9), and challenged God's providence (10:10). In other words, they failed because their actions did not correspond with their so-called "faith." Again, the unmistakable implication for the Corinthians (and, by extrapolation, for all Christians) is that they too might fail if their practice of the faith did not measure up to their knowledge of the faith.

This is the earliest statement we have against what might be called sacramental presumption (presuming that one is saved simply because one "has" the sacraments). The fact that this warning had to be given so early within the history of the Church—within scarcely more than a generation of Jesus' death and Resurrection—witnesses to that sad tendency of human nature to turn a living relationship with God into a matter of having done the right rituals. In this way the sacraments which are, in reality, living encounters with a living God who wants the *whole* of us for himself—body, mind, and soul— become, instead, empty formalities through which we attempt to keep God at a safe distance, to limit him to a narrow, "sacred" sphere.

Apparently some of the Corinthians were tempted to make their faith mostly a matter of externals. The same temptation applies to Christians today, as is evident from this stern warning (written in the spirit of St. Paul!) addressed to us by the Second Vatican Council in its *Dogmatic Constitution on the Church* (Chapter 2, Article 14):

> He is not saved, however, who, though he is part of the body of the Church, does not persevere in charity. He remains indeed in the bosom of the Church, but, as it were, only in a "bodily" manner and not "in the heart." All the sons of the Church should remember that their exalted status is to be attributed not to their own merits but to the special grace of Christ. If they fail moreover to respond to that grace in thought, word, and deed, not only will they not be saved but they will be the more severely judged.

Paul sums up the import of these Old Testament illustrations in 10:12—they are a warning against spiritual pride and self-sufficiency, whether from one's superior "knowledge," through a mechanistic and magical misunderstanding of the sacraments, or from one's distinguished pedigree as a Jewish Christian. There is really no excuse, he continues in 10:13, for a Christian to express this kind of prideful arrogance in attitude or action. After all, all Christians, by the fact of their humanity, are subject to such temptations. But we know that we can overcome these temptations by responding to God's grace. God's grace will always be sufficient to meet any situation. He says this to remind and, in the process of reminding, to empower some of the Corinthian Christians to make certain changes in their lives.

Apparently some of the "knowledgeable" (those who indulged in sacrificial meat because of their "superior" understanding) not only were eating meat which previously had been offered to idols, but were taking part in the actual sacrifice. Undoubtedly they claimed immunity in doing this; after all, they were Christians and idols no longer existed for them. Paul strongly objected to what they were doing. The reasons for his objection, given in 10:14-22, give us invaluable insight into how the very early Church understood the celebration of the Lord's Supper, or Eucharist.

Paul starts this section in a strongly personal, strongly authoritative way. At the same time he affirms his love and demands a change in behavior (10:14). The Greek of 10:14b is expressed in the strongest possible terms. It reads literally "flee from idolatry!" The patent reasonableness of the argument that follows is underlined in 10:15.

The disputation proper begins with two rhetorical questions (10:16); that is, questions whose answers are so obvious that the answer is already contained in the process of asking the question. This in itself is significant, because it illustrates that the celebration of the Eucharist was already so well-established that Paul could simply presume its meaning in his discussion.

The "cup of blessing" (10:16) was the liturgical term for the third toast offered at the Passover meal, just after the eating of the paschal lamb. The use of this term by Paul shows that the very early Church viewed the Eucharist in the context of Passover. Scholarly debate still persists over whether the Last Supper was celebrated at the actual time of Passover, (following the tradition of Mark, Matthew, and Luke) or the day before (following the tradition of John). This author maintains that Jesus was certainly creative and daring enough to move *his* celebration of Passover up a day! At any rate, the Passover connotation of "cup of blessing" is unmistakable. "Cup of blessing *we bless*" (10:16a) is a curious redundancy on Paul's part, *unless* the "we bless" refers to a solemn act/attitude of consecration. The element of solemn blessing, or consecration, points to a sacrificial context for the celebration of this meal, since such a consecration was an important part of both Jewish and pagan sacrificial offerings. The aspect of sacrifice becomes inescapable when we combine this with the "cup of blessing" reference to Passover (with its own sacrificial connotations) and the identification (through double use of the verb *is*) of the sacred elements with "sharing in" Christ.

The Greek word *koinonia*, which is variously translated as "sharing in" (NAB), "communion with" (JB), or "participation in" (RSV), was often used in contemporary writings of the time to express the intimacy of the marriage relationship or, in a sacrificial context, the union of the worshipper with the god being worshipped. The fact that Paul uses this word in a Eucharistic setting points to a real identification on his part between Christ and the Christian which happens (*relationally*, not mechanically!) in the celebration of this rite. In other words, Christ, for Paul, was really, tangibly present in the celebration of the Lord's Supper.

The word *koinonia* is the root of the Greek words for community and fellowship. Theologically speaking, communion with Christ spills over into community with fellow Christians. That Paul was thinking along these lines is evident from 10:17 (which is about community) following 10:16 (which is about communion). This verse (10:17) is a notable development of his understanding of the "Mystical Body." We have seen how, in 6:13b-20, he unfolded the reality of the individual Christian being incorporated into the "Body of Christ." Here, in 10:17, he expands this reality to include an essential communal dimension. Sharing in the Eucharist simultaneously effects two kinds of communion: the communion of the individual Christian with his Lord, and the communion of Christian with Christian through their mutual relationship with their common Lord. Thus, is a very real sense the Body of Christ is *one*, one because Christ is one, and his presence enables us to be at one with each other.

Paul pursues his argument by making a striking connection

between both Jewish and pagan sacrifices and the sacrificial nature of the Eucharist. "Israel according to the flesh" (10:18a) refers to the "old" Israel in contrast to the "new" Israel, which is the Church. Paul cites the typically Jewish view of sacrifice, which is that the person who eats of the sacrificial offering becomes connected to the intent of that offering. Thus, for example, to sincerely partake of a peace offering carried with it the effect of becoming at peace with Yahweh. "Sharing in the altar" (10:18b) was another way of saying to become reconciled with Yahweh, since Yahweh was believed to be present at his altar. Thus, in this verse Paul is simply describing the character of the Jewish sacrificial system.

He switches abruptly to his real concern—pagan sacrifices (those in which some of the Corinthian Christians were participating)—and is quick to admit (as the "knowledgeable" themselves maintained) that idols are really nothing (10:19). *But*, Paul continues in 10:20, even though the gods behind the idols may be nothing, idolatrous worship of this kind is not really nonpartisan. Ultimately it is an act of identification with the devil, because the evil one lurks behind all false worship.

Paul has carefully assembled his trap. He springs it in 10:21 with his jolting statement of the absolute incompatibility between participating in pagan sacrifice and sharing in the sacrifice of Christ in the Eucharist. His choice to the "knowledgeable" of Corinth (and, by projection, to the "knowledgeable" of today) is one of either/or.

Either they choose to continue to take part in pagan sacrifices, thus defiling themselves by the very real identification which takes place at that altar between the devil and his followers; or they choose to limit themselves to communing with Christ at his altar, finding salvation in the very real relationship expressed through his body and blood. They cannot have it *both* ways. Paul speaks of the Lord as being "jealous" in 10:22, reminding the Corinthians of the intimate nature of their relationship with Christ, a relationship in which identification with anyone else in worship is spiritual adultery in the same sense as is sexual union with a prostitute (discussed in 6:13b-20).

To summarize: this section (10:14-22) is a decisive one for understanding Paul's attitude (and, by implication, the attitude of the very early Church) toward the Eucharist. Two crucial aspects of the Lord's Supper are highlighted in this part of his letter: that of sacrifice and that of community. His understanding of sacrifice has been shaped by the sacrificial traditions of the Old Testament. He does not criticize or correct the Old Testament in this regard; rather, he replaces the multitude of Old Testament sacrifices with the one true sacrifice of Christ.

For Paul, and for the early Church in general, Passion Week is one great act of Sacrifice on the part of Jesus. The Last Supper and the crucifixion were seen not so much as two separate events, but as complementary and interdependent parts of the same sacrificial reality. Thus, in a profound sense the reality of the crucifixion was already present at the Last Supper, just as the reality of the Last Supper was itself continued in the crucifixon. Indeed, the early Church subsumed both these sacrificial events into the larger reality of the Resurrection, since it was the Resurrection which endowed both the Last Supper and the crucifixion with saving power.

When the early Church blessed, or consecrated, the bread and the wine as the body and blood of Christ, it was offering to the Father the only really effective sacrifice, that of Jesus himself. The Church did not consider itself to be re-crucifying Jesus with each celebration of the Eucharist. Instead, the Eucharistic sacrifice enabled the Christian community to participate in the one true sacrifice of Calvary. This participation, or communion, was seen in very real terms; a person actually received the Lord in the sacred elements. Christ's presence in the bread and wine was real; for it to be experienced as real. however, presupposed a personal relationship between the believer and Christ. In other words, the Eucharist was seen as a kind of intensification of an already very real relationship between Christ and the believer. It was not understood as automatically saving someone who was not already in a saving relationship with the Lord.

The Lord's Supper was the great common act of worship which brought all Christians together. Indeed, assuming a genuineness of faith in each individual Christian, the real—and shared—presence of the Lord in the Eucharist was what transformed an incongruous assortment of individual Christians into an organic and organized community. In this case, the whole was incomparably greater than the sum of its parts, because it was the community as a whole which became the Body of Christ.

Having answered the question of whether or not it was permissible for a Christian to take part in pagan sacrifices with a resounding "No!", Paul goes on to answer the other questions which the Corinthians had asked him regarding the topic of idol-meat. Returning to the refrain about everything being lawful (which, as we remember from our discussion of 6:12, is his own shorthand which has been turned against him), he repeats it twice (10:23), each time with a qualification which directs freedom beyond itself to love. He expands these qualifications into a general principle in 10:24, "No man should seek his own interest but rather that of his neighbor," a principle which states in a straightforward way what was said in a less direct way in 8:9 and 8:13. This general principle serves to review and to sum up his underlying attitude on this matter.

From the general he turns to the specific in 10:25. His point is that Christians need have no scruples about buying meat in the public market (even if it has been part of an idol-offering), because the offering, in itself, does not affect the Christian and since, in the context of private consumption, no scandal or stumbling block is involved. He quotes (10:26) from Psalm 24:1 to affirm the Christian belief that in reality everything is the Lord's (even if it has been sacrificed to idols).

Next, Paul gives his permission to attend dinner parties in the homes of non-Christian friends (10:27), provided that no one says anything about the food having been sacrificed to idols. If someone does, it automatically becomes more than a personal issue, and the Christian must abstain (10:28-29a). This is a clear instance when one's own preference must be surrendered for the good of the community (10:29b-30).

Paul draws this whole long section (8:1-11:1) to a close by recasting his general principle in yet another way in 10:31—"Whatever you do—you should do all for the glory of God." He gathers in some of the other strands of his extended argument (such as becoming all things to all men) in 10:32-33, and once again asks the Corinthian Christians to follow his own example, because in doing so they will be following the example of Christ (11:1).

Questions for Personal Reflection/Group Discussion:

1. What is sacramental presumption?
2. How and why has sacramental presumption been a major temptation in the Catholic Church?
3. What indications are there in Paul's text that the Eucharist was celebrated largely as a sacrifice by the early Church?
4. (a)Although people no longer literally make offerings to idols, it has been suggested that our society—including many Christians— is still very much involved with idol worship. How might this be so?

   (b) What are some modern idols—false realities which today are just as incompatible with the sacrifice of the Eucharist as idol-meat was in Paul's day?
5. How are Eucharist and community interrelated?

Chapter 15: Responsibilities and Realities Connected to Christian Worship I: Appropriate Attire and Behavior at Church

Please read 1 Corinthians 11:2-16. Not only had Paul been informed of certain deficiencies regarding the practice of morality in the

Corinthian church; he had been told of certain irregularities in their worship as well. The next four chapters (11-14) deal with issues relating to public worship. In this section (11:2-34) he deals with the problem of women who refused to cover their heads in church. As is so much of this letter, we shall see that although his specific advice may be dated, his underlying concerns and principles most certainly are not. Avoiding public scandal is as important today as it was two thousand years ago.

Paul begins by tactfully thanking the Corinthians for their remembrance, both of him personally and of the tradition which he had passed on to them (11:2). "Traditions" refers to authoritative teachings, both oral and written, in the areas of faith, worship, and morals. Immediately after this polite introduction Paul plunges into the heart of his argument. The problem was that some of the women in the Corinthian church had begun participating in public worship with their heads uncovered. Perhaps they, too, considered themselves too "knowledgeable" to abide by this custom. Complications arose from the fact that in Corinth the only women who appeared in public without veils were prostitutes. Thus, Christian women who rejected the veil were causing public scandal. In addition to bringing bad reputations upon themselves, they were providing the opportunity for the non-Christians in the city to wonder what was really going on in Christian worship.

Paul's concern is much more centered on the problem of scandal than it is on the precise role of Christian women. To be sure, he uses some strongly theological reasoning to prove his point. His theology on this issue, however, is a curious mixture of metaphysical presuppositions and cultural preconceptions. The fact that hardly a Christian church today continues to enforce his ruling that women must keep their heads covered in church, suggests that Christianity as a whole has recognized that Paul's major concern here was, indeed, scandal, and not some ecclesiastical ruling intended to stand for all time. In our day (except in some Near Eastern and Eastern cultures where such reasoning would still apply) the question of whether or not women cover their heads is no longer a moral issue; therefore Paul's concern for scandal—and the ruling it engendered—no longer apply.

At any rate, Paul wields his heaviest argument first; no less than a claim that the nature of existence is hierarchical (11:3). This statement is a revealed truth and is therefore authoritative; it cannot be changed to conform to differing opinions on the roles of men and women. The fact that this is a revealed truth, however, actually places it beyond the realm of argumentation. It is too abstract to draw from it (at least in any kind of logical way) the complex mixture of observation and legislation which he himself does in 11:4-10. In other words, his specific conclusions do not necessarily follow from his general theological principle in 11:3. This is precisely why his specific ruling was capable of being changed without contradicting Scripture.

Paul switches from using "head" in a metaphysical way in 11:3 to using it in a literal way in 11:4-10. According to him, a man is supposed to pray with his head uncovered (11:4) so as to be able to reflect God's glory (11:7a). Because of her unique place in the order of creation (11:7b), a place which he sees here as definitely secondary to man's (11:8-9), a woman who prays with her head uncovered offends her proper dignity and usurps the place of the man (11:5). Paul indulges in some sarcasm in 11:6. "The angels" in 11:10 is an allusion to the Jewish belief, current in his time, that angels witnessed the liturgy, and that these angels would be offended at the impropriety of bareheaded women.

It seems obvious that Paul himself is not terribly pleased with the coherence of his argument, given the surprising twist in 11:11-12. His "yet" (which can also be translated as "nevertheless" or "however") seems to betray a certain uneasiness on his part. After concentrating so heavily on woman's subordination to man, he now gives a startling expression of equality, reminiscent of his "There does not exist among you Jew or Greek, slave or freeman, male or female" in Galatians 3:28. He doesn't know what to do with this insight, however (which is just as true of his theological statement in 11:3), and quickly goes back to throwing out more reasons for women having to wear the veil (11:13-15). His argument from ''nature'' in 11:14 is particularly unconvincing, seeing how ''nature'' has inspired different fashions in different times and places. His final word on this matter (11:16) is more substantive, appealing as it does to authority, his own in the context of that of the Church.

In our discussion of the ''danger of fossilization'' (p. 55) we saw how the Holy Spirit is able to inspire the Church to new ways of approaching truths which are, in themselves, unchanging. The same process of continuing inspiration and insight through the Holy Spirit is helpful in this context of apostolic authority. Ecclesiastical legislation (such as this ruling of Paul's about Chrisian women having to keep their heads covered) is given for the sake of building up the Body of Christ. It was never intended to be like the edicts of the Persian emperors which, once stated, could never be changed. Thus, given the reality of real guidance under the leadership of the Holy Spirit, it is perfectly consistent—even necessary—for the same truths to be expressed in different ways in different periods throughout the history of the Church.

The basic concern in this section is with the duty of Christians to avoid scandal (except, of course, in the sense that a Christian's primary relationship to Christ is always rather scandalous to the world-at-large). In every age the Church assumes that part of the Christian vocation is to be a good example to the world in which one lives. The precise content of what constitutes a good example may differ from age to age, but the basic calling remains the same. Certain Christian women in Corinth were bringing with them into the Christian community moral scandal instead of moral approbation. Paul corrects the situation for the good of the Church.

In addition to the general moral principle at stake (avoiding scandal), this section of Paul's letter (11:2-16) is particularly interesting because it raises the whole question of the proper specificity of theology. In other words, how far can one legitimately go in terms of drawing specific conclusions from theological principles? We have seen that he went too far with his inferences from 11:3; the conclusions concerning the proper behavior of women did not follow from his theological premise. Such a potent example of fallacious inference should alert us to the peril of using theology to ''prove'' a point which, on closer examination, is seen to be a cultural bias. Thus, for example, it does *not* follow from the theological truth that ''the head of a woman is her husband'' (11:3b) that she is therefore inferior to her husband (and should be assigned to ''lower'' positions in ministry, etc.) just as it does not follow from the theological truth that ''the head of Christ is the Father'' (11:3c) that Christ is therefore inferior to the Father. We need to be as careful not to read too much into Scripture as we must be to find within it all that it really intends to say!

Question for Personal Reflection/Group Discussion:

1. Can you think of any other false conclusions drawn from correct theological premises? Be prepared to defend the logic of your reasoning!

Chapter 16:   Responsibilities and Realities Connected to Christian Worship II: The Meaning of the Eucharist

Please read I Corinthians 11:17-34.   The factionalism of the Corinthian church extended even to its celebration of the Lord's Supper. Paul's censure in this section exposes a situation in which the Corinthians would carry theological and economic differences with them right into their most solemn act of public worship. In the Christian community at Corinth at this time the Eucharist was celebrated after a common meal had been shared by the participants. This common meal was similar to a modern day potluck. Different people would bring different dishes according to their inclination and their means.

Unfortunately the ''common'' element of these common meals had been lost. The preliminary meal had degenerated from fellowship based on love (an *agapé* meal) to a free-for-all in which everyone did as they pleased. Thus, some of the well-to-do would bring fancy food and hurry to eat it so that they would not have to share with the poor. Individuals belonging to a particular faction would sit together, disdaining those whose opinions differed from theirs. Some would even get drunk waiting for the Eucharist to begin. The picture Paul paints in 11:17-22 is a dismal one; so dismal, in fact, that Paul bluntly tells the Corinthians that "When you assemble it is not to eat the Lord's Supper" (11:20). Their disgraceful conduct at the "common" meal was undermining the real meaning of the Eucharist.

The shameful way in which the Corinthians have been treating the Lord's Supper prompts Paul to recall for them the real meaning of this act (11:23-26). This is the earliest account of the Eucharist which we have in the New Testament, antedating that of Mark's Gospel by approximately a decade. The magnitude of this legacy is mirrored in Paul's solemn introduction: "I received from the Lord what I handed on to you . . . " (11:23a). This twofold process of (1) receiving from the Lord and (2) the content of what was received, was what the early Church called Tradition.

Containing both a written dimension (that is, Scripture, which at this time meant the Old Testament, because the New Testament was still being written) and an oral dimension, Tradition was the highest form of authoritative teaching within the Christian community. The whole sense of Tradition was that it was teaching of such fundamental importance that it had to be handed on from generation to generation intact, unaltered in any of its essentials. What alarmed Paul so much concerning the Corinthian "celebration" of the Lord's Supper was precisely the fact that their divisive attitudes and actions were, indeed, altering the true meaning of the Eucharist. The Corinthians were turning the Lord's Supper into a celebration of divisions rather than a celebration of unity and community. In short, the Corinthians needed to be reminded of some of the fundamentals of their faith, and this is what Paul sets out to do in these verses (11:23-26).

". . . The Lord Jesus on the night in which he was betrayed took bread'' (11:23b), in addition to reflecting the words of institution of a very early Christian liturgy, is also, of course, a historical memory which links each celebration of the Lord's Supper to the original celebration of the Lord's Supper. The Christian understanding of historical memory, or remembrance, was the same as that of the Jews. In fact, what the early Christians did was to take the Jewish understanding of their great feasts, such as Passover, and to make it the normative Christian approach to the Eucharist (and, by extension, to the rest of the sacraments).

For the Jewish people, to celebrate or remember Passover was not merely a process of mentally recalling a past historical event; it was the process of participating in the truth of that historical event in the reality of the present. Thus, to remember Passover was to participate in the abiding truth of the first Passover; it was, literally, to re-member the Exodus experience into the here-and-now, to celebrate it as a *present* saving reality, and not just as a past historical event.

This was precisely the attitude of the early Christians toward the Eucharist (and continues to be the attitude of present-day Catholicism). To remember the Last Supper did not mean to look back to the original event as a past historical memory, but to open oneself to the present, saving reality of that event. We need to keep in mind here an important distinction between the original event and the re-enactment or re-presentation of the event in such liturgical celebrations as Passover and the Eucharist. There was one actual, historical Passover just as Jesus celebrated the Last Supper or First Eucharist once, and there was one actual, historical sacrifice of Christ on Calvary. To participate in Passover or the Eucharist does not mean that we are repeating past history (literally recrossing the Sea or recrucifying Jesus), but that we are allowing the eternal truth of that past event to become present for us. Thus, the sacrifice we offer at the Eucharist is the one, same sacrifice of Jesus at Calvary. Our offering of Christ in the present is only possible because the reality of Jesus' sacrifice back then was saving and effective for *all* time.

''And after he had given thanks, broke it and said, 'This is my body, which is for you. Do this in remembrance of me.' " (11:24). The thanksgiving, or blessing, was said over the third cup at the Passover meal. The fact that Paul uses the phrase "after he had given thanks" indicates that the early Church (in the Tradition of Jesus himself) understood the Last Supper in the context of Passover, with its sacrificial connotations. Moreover, the fact that the bread was *broken*, and that it was expressly broken *for you*, also point to a sacrificial understanding of the Lord's Supper. Furthermore, the reality of Jesus' sacrificial death links up with the Suffering Servant imagery of Isaiah, especially Isaiah 53. Doing this—eating the eucharistic bread with faith and commitment—remembers Christ precisely in the Jewish sense of making him present now. Thus, Jesus is really present in the eucharistic bread. To eat the bread is to commune with the Lord.

" 'This cup is the new covenant in my blood' " (11:25b), continues the theme of sacrifice, and extends the imagery of the Eucharist to include the concept of covenant. God's offer of covenant is one of the major themes of the Old Testament. A covenant was essentially a sequence of promises between two parties pledging fidelity to one another. Thus, in the context of the Old Testament, God would always take the initiative and promise himself to his people who, in turn, would promise loyalty to him. Covenant was often connected to sacrifice, the sacrifice being the action which ratified the covenant. There is a powerful example of this connection in Exodus 24:7-8 (in which Moses is mediating a renewal of the covenant between God and his people), a passage which is echoed at the Lord's Supper:

> Taking the book of the covenant, he read it aloud to the people, who answered, "All that the Lord has said, we will heed and do." Then he took the blood and sprinkled it on the people, saying, "This is the *blood of the covenant* which the LORD has made with you in accordance with all these words of his."

The problem with covenant in the Old Testament is that it kept having to be repeated. The prophets yearned for a new covenant, one which would be truly effective in establishing a love relationship between God and his people: "The days are coming, says the LORD, when I will make a new covenant with the house of Israel and the house of Judah" (Jeremiah 31:31). Again, the Lord's Supper picks up on the theme of a *new* covenant; this time, however, not as an echo, but as the *fulfillment* of the yearning expressed in the "old" covenant: " 'This cup *is* the new covenant in my blood' " (11:25).

According to the Eucharist, then, Jesus' sacrificial death brings about the new covenant—the possibility of a qualitatively new, and lasting, relationship between God and people. Access to this new covenant is through joining the Lord at his Last Supper. Drinking this cup in "remembrance" Jesus, for the person of true faith and commitment, means nothing less than meeting the real presence of Christ in the cup of his blood. To drink the wine is to commune with the Lord.

Paul considers two more dimensions of the Eucharist in 11:26. The first of these is the element of proclamation, which echoes the Jewish practice (again, the Passover celebration would be a good example of this) of recounting God's saving deeds with joy and thanksgiving. (Significantly, the verb *eucharistia* in Greek means joyful thanksgiving.) A good part of the content of the Church's eucharistic prayers, both ancient and modern, has been just such a thankful remembering of God's saving deeds, culminating with the life, sacrifice, and Resurrection of Jesus. The context of the Lord's Supper is so overwhelming that its content literally overflows into the joyful proclamation of God's goodness and love.

The second aspect of the Eucharist which Paul mentions in 11:26 is that of expectancy at the Lord's return. This element, one having to do with eschatology—teachings on the last things—catapults us into the future, when Christ will come again. In this setting the phrase "you proclaim the death of the Lord until he comes" (11:26b) is a profound profession of faith (in Jesus' saving death) which spills over into hope (his coming again). From the viewpoint of eschatology, the Eucharist is a present glimpse into the future reality of heaven, a promise of the great heavenly banquet which is already on its way.

Paul finishes his fundamental teaching on the Eucharist with 11:26. He proceeds to draw some conclusions from his teaching (11:27-34). Because the Eucharist is the supreme act of worship on this planet, those who approach it frivolously (as many of the Corinthians were doing) are commiting a serious sin. Notice the parallelism in 11:27 between bread and body, cup and blood: another indication that Paul and the early Church considered Jesus to be really present in the Eucharist. Surely he would not have labeled lack of respect for a merely symbolic presence as sinning against the "body and blood of the Lord."

Since the Lord's Supper is a personal communion with the Lord, it is essential to prepare oneself beforehand (11:28). Such preparation in the early Church probably included (as it still should today) examining one's conscience. asking for forgiveness, and reflecting on the significance of what one is about to do. So important is the realization that one is communing with the real Christ, that Paul categorically states in 11:29 that the person who participates in the Lord's Supper without "recognizing the body" ("body" meaning both the real presence of Christ in the Eucharist and in the Christian community) is "eating and drinking his own condemnation" (*Jerusalem Bible*). He goes on to attribute much of the sickness and death within the Corinthian church to their abuses of the Lord's Supper (11:30-32). He concludes this part of his letter with advice designed to restore order to their eucharistic celebrations (11:33-34).

This section of Paul's letter, together with 5:7b and 10:14-22, comprises his official teaching on the meaning of the Lord's Supper. These are the only references to the Eucharist in his letters, a surprising fact which seems to point to the "breaking of the Bread" as such a basic part of Christian life that it was somewhat taken for granted, much like the air we breathe. We are fortunate to have his teaching on this matter. Without it our understanding of the meaning and importance of the Lord's Supper in the very early Church would be much poorer. Given the incredible fullness of meaning of Paul's understanding of the Eucharist—a fullness of meaning which includes the dimensions of sacrifice, community, covenant, proclamation-thanksgiving, and eschatology—we can see that both those who have turned it into a mechanical grace-dispenser and those who have turned it into an abstract symbol are equally far from the truth.

Questions for Personal Reflection/Group Discussion:

1. What facts indicate that St. Paul taught the real presence of Christ in the Eucharist?
2. At this point in your spiritual life, which dimension of the Eucharist means the most to you personally? Why?
3. Which dimension of the Eucharist would you like to participate in more fully? Why?

Chapter 17: Maturing in the Gifts of the Spirit I: Unity and Community

Please read 1 Corinthians 12. Up to this point, Paul has been dealing largely with the "worldly" elements within the Corinthian church, those who could too easily rationalize sexual immorality, lawsuits, eating meat which had been offered to idols. Now he takes on the "spiritual" circles within the Christian community at Corinth, those who considered themselves superior because of the alleged superiority of their spiritual gifts. Not a few Christians in Corinth gravitated toward those spiritual gifts which are most outwardly spectacular, gifts such as speaking in tongues and healing.

Paul never puts down any of the spiritual gifts, but he does insist that they be exercised for the good of the entire community (and not merely for the edification of individuals or private interest groups), and that they be kept in perspective through the higher standard of love. In chapter 12 he highlights the unifying role of the Holy Spirit, presents his analogy of the body, and further develops his image of the

Body of Christ. Chapter 13 praises love as both the greatest spiritual gift and the one without which the rest of the gifts would be meaningless. Guidelines for the practice of some of the more dramatic gifts are given in chapter 14.

Paul opens his discussion by reminding many of the Corinthians of their recent pagan pasts (12:2), pasts which often involved participation in frenzied mystery cults, and which sometimes still erupted into blasphemy (12:3a). He reminds these pagan converts that the Holy Spirit does not speak in contradictions; the Spirit would never inspire anyone to insult the name of Jesus. Indeed, the very recognition that "Jesus is Lord" (that is, savior and ruler of one's life) is itself an inspiration of the Holy Spirit (12:3b).

In the next section (12:4-11) Paul underlines the role of the Holy Spirit as unifier of the Christian community. Note that he does not stress the action of the Holy Spirit to the exclusion of Christ and the Father; his threefold citation of "Spirit," "Lord," and "God" in 12:4-6 shows that he thought of the three as equal in identity but complementary in function. It is the unique role of the Holy Spirit as vivifier and unifier of the community that he wants to emphasize in this section.

Before listing some of the gifts of the Holy Spirit, Paul states unequivocally that the sole purpose of any spiritual gift is to build up the community (12:7). This statement, plus the fact that the gifts are distributed at "random" in 12:11 (we cannot claim any credit for them), serves to counteract the excessively individualistic attitude with which the Corinthians had been approaching the gifts.

The spiritual gifts which Paul lists in 12:8-10 can be described as follows: "wisdom in discourse" is the ability to articulate deep spiritual truths; "the power to express knowledge" means being able to apply this wisdom to the everyday life of the community; "faith" in this context goes way beyond belief—it refers to that effective faith which is able to "move mountains" (see, for example, Mark 11:23); "healing" means healing, both physical and what we would call psychological; "miraculous powers" probably refers to the ability to perform exorcisms; "prophecy" is the faculty of discerning God's will for the present; "power to distinguish one spirit from another" is the ability to discern true from false prophecy; "the gift of tongues" is that of ecstatic, unintelligible prayer; "interpreting the tongues" is being able to make the unintelligible intelligible.

The number and diversity of the gifts which Paul mentions in these three verses witnesses to the depth and breadth of Christian life in the church at Corinth. It also gives us an idea of the magnitude of the problem which he was having to deal with, considering that many individuals were claiming that their particular gifts were superior to all others.

The analogy of the body (12:12-26) addresses the problem of the competitiveness within the Corinthian church through the use of a simple, but powerful, image. Teaching by way of analogy was highly effective. The image provided something concrete to hang on to, and it could easily be recalled. Perhaps even more importantly, analogies encouraged a more organic type of learning, one in which living, relational interconnections could more easily be made.

Paul leads off his analogy by outlining the connections to be made (12:12). Notice the progression of his thought here from "body" through "many members" back to "one body": body = one = many members; many members = one body. The crucial point is stated in the last part of the verse (12:12c): "and so it is with Christ." There is an analogical correspondence, in other words, between the human body, which is a basic unity even though made up of many different parts, and the Body of Christ—the Church—which is also a basic unity composed of many different members. The power which enables this unity is none other than the Holy Spirit (12:13). To be baptised means nothing less than to receive the Holy Spirit and to become a living member of the Body of Christ, a member radically at one with all other members of Christ's Body because the Spirit shared is one.

The body part of the analogy is now developed at length (12:14-26). To get its full flavor, it must be read in the context of the absurd competitiveness of the Corinthian church regarding which of the gifts is the greatest. In this setting, Paul's observation in 12:22, "Even those members of the body which seem less important are in fact indispensable," and in 12:26, "If one member suffers, all the members suffer with it; if one member is honored, all the members share its joy" take on new significance as personal challenges to the Corinthian Christians to respect and appreciate one another.

In 12:27 Paul, for the first time in any of his letters, makes a direct equation between the Christian community and the Body of Christ: "You, then, *are* the body of Christ." This equation includes within it the individual as a vital part of this body: "Every one of you is a member of it." Note that Paul does not speak in terms of simile ("You are *like* the body of Christ"), but in terms of actuality ("You *are* the body of Christ), terms which echo Jesus' equation of the bread with his body ("This *is* my body") and the wine with his blood ("This *is* my blood").

To dampen the overemphasis of the Corinthian church on the outwardly impressive gifts, such as speaking in tongues, Paul sets up a hierarchy of spiritual gifts in which speaking in tongues takes last place (12:28). What is described in this and the next three verses (12:29-31a) is an important difference between *function* (in which some roles can be described as being "greater" than others), and *identity* (in which all Christians share a basic equality in the Lord). At this point Paul drops everything to describe the greatest gift of all (12:31b).

Questions for Personal Reflection/Group Discussion:

1. What theological truth is Paul communicating by equating the Christian community with the Body of Christ?
2. What spiritual gifts have you been given, and how do you use them to build up the Christian community?

**Chapter 18:   Maturing in the Gifts of the Spirit II:
Love as the Greatest Gift**

Please read I Corinthians 13. Paul's magnificent meditation on love—is one of the best known and most treasured chapters in the entire Bible. It is a passionate and poetic series of insights into the sum and substance of the Greek *agapé*, the uniquely Christian term for love. *Agapé* was actually a rather lowly word until adopted by Christianity. It was not a very common word, and described only mildly affectionate gratitude. Much more commonly used were the other Greek words for love: *erós*, passionate attraction; *storgé*, family attachment; and *philia*, intimate friendship.

None of these quite captured the precise nuance that Christianity wished to communicate, so Christian authors simply took over this Greek word and transformed its meaning. The meaning they bestowed on *agapé* was that of God's unconditional love for humanity, a love which was not conditioned by anything a person did or failed to do, a love so graciously and spontaneously given on God's part that it inspired people to respond in kind. In other words, the only really adequate way of thanking God for his *agapé* for us is to demonstrate *agapé* toward others. This kind of unconditional love, then, is the form of love about which Paul speaks so eloquently in this chapter.

His vision of love needs to be seen within the larger context of chapters 12-14. Love is by far the greatest, the most God-reflecting, of the spiritual gifts. As such it is the most needed gift within the Christian community. This chapter is not just a beautiful poem, but an impassioned plea for *all* Christians to begin loving one another in the same way in which Christ loves us. Paul's "model" for this chapter was Jesus. Who else could he have looked to for such a simple, complete, and inspiring picture of what it truly means to love?

Paul's poem is carefully structured in three roughly equal parts: the first section (13:1-3) describes the worthlessness of all the other spiritual gifts without a motivation in love; the second section (13:4-7) describes the character of love; the third section (13:8-13) describes the transcendent nature of love.

He begins with the spiritual gift which had degenerated into a symbol of self-centered superiority for some of the Corinthians—that of speaking in tongues (1:1). They considered themselves better than others—elevated almost to the status of angels because they spoke an "angelic" tongue—because they had been blessed with this gift. Paul compares speaking in tongues which is not motivated by agapic love—love of God which overflows into love for one's neighbor—to the meaningless noise of pagan temple worship. In 13:2 he considers the gifts of prophecy and faith, again reducing them to worthlessness without a foundation in love. Likewise, in 13:3, even powerfully good actions like sacrificial giving and martyrdom amount to nothing apart from the prior gift of love.

In the short second section of his meditation, Paul names no fewer than fourteen different, but complementary aspects of love. It is impossible to capture the powerful flow of this section in English, since we have to use adjectives and nouns to translate what are all verbal forms in the original Greek. According to St. Paul, the decisive characteristics of true Christian love are the following:

1. "Love is patient"—the word used for "patient" is the specific Greek word for patience with *people*. The Christian, in other words, is supposed to image God's long-suffering love toward him toward others.

2. "Love is kind"—the meaning here is that Christian love is warmly relational to others. It is empathetic and compassionate.

3. "Love is not jealous"—jealousy and love are incompatible because jealousy reaches in through possessiveness, while love reaches out through sharing.

4. "It does not put on airs"—it looks not to its own self-importance, but to service.

5. "It is not snobbish"—the loving person does not consider himself or herself to be better than others. Love is not arrogant.

6. "Love is never rude"—this phrase could be translated "Love is not without grace," grace in this context referring to graciousness.

7. "It is not self-seeking"—in other words, true Christian love embodies sacrifice, not selfishness.

8. "It is not prone to anger"—it does not "take offence" (JB); is not "irritable" (RSV).

9. "Neither does it brood over injuries"—the word for "brood" could also be rendered as "store up." This was a term used in accounting, and in this setting gives the sense of meticulously keeping track of wrongs suffered. Love does not nurse resentment, but offers forgiveness.

10. "Love does not rejoice in what is wrong but rejoices with the truth"—it does not delight in seeing the moral stumblings or falls of others. Love is not self-righteous.

11. "There is no limit to love's forebearance"—it resists the temptation to jump to judgment.

12. "To its trust"—love goes on believing in God and in people no matter what.

13. "Its hope"—love will never give up expecting that things *will* work out for the best.

14. "Its power to endure"—the meaning of "to endure" in Greek is not passive, but active in the sense of overcoming something through endurance. Love, in other words, conquers all.

Paul speaks of the invincible power of love in the third part of his vision. "Love never fails" (13:8a) can also be translated as "Love does not come to an end" (JB). This statement serves to contrast the eternal, perfect nature of love with the temporal and imperfect nature of all the other spiritual gifts (13:8-9). The "perfect" which is coming (13:10) is the fullness of the Kingdom of God, a fullness which will embody the gift of love, but which will have no need of the other spiritual gifts. To illustrate his point, Paul employs the metaphor of human growth and development (13:11). Just as an adult is a qualitatively different being from a child, the fullness of the Kingdom—in which love will play a central role—will be immeasurably more intense and real than what we are able to experience of the Kingdom now.

Paul switches his metaphor to one of seeing in 13:12. Just as the rather crude polished metal mirrors of the time weren't altogether successful in reflecting the human image, neither is our theological knowledge (or, for that matter, the other spiritual gifts) really an adequate reflector of God's already perfect knowledge of us. Paul's parallel expressions ''then we shall see face to face'' and ''then I shall know even as I am known'' give us a wonderful glimpse as to what lies ahead of us in the fullness of God's Kingdom. The first part of 13:13, ''There are in the end three things that last: faith, hope, and love'' was already a cliché in Paul's time. His addition of ''and the greatest of these is love'' transforms this commonplace into a part of Paul's mystical vision.

The sheer descriptive power of this incredible chapter must have had a profound effect on at least some of the Corinthian Christians. So many of their attitudes and actions, narrated earlier in this letter, were such serious contradictions, or countersigns, to the vision of love presented here, that one cannot help but think that this chapter stopped them in their tracks and made them reconsider the depth of their commitment to Christ. Let us hope that Paul's powerful words will have the same effect on us.

Questions for Personal Reflection/Group Discussion:

1. Why is love the greatest spiritual gift?
2. Which aspect of love would you say that you are strongest in? Weakest in?

Chapter 19:   Maturing in the Gifts of the Spirit III: The Community Comes First

Please read I Corinthians 14. This chapter gives us some fascinating insights into the practice of the Liturgy of the Word in the very early Church. We know that the Liturgy of the Word was observed at a different time from that of the common meal and the Liturgy of the Eucharist, because visitors were allowed to be present at the former, but not at the latter.

The picture we get of this primitive Liturgy of the Word is one of great informality and spontaneity. Indeed, this element of Christian worship among the Corinthians was apparently just as chaotic as their celebration of the Lord's Supper, since Paul had to attend to some serious abuses here, as he had done already in connection with the Eucharist. The picture we get of the Liturgy of the Word at Corinth is not just one of informality and spontaneity, but one of confusion and uproar. People were speaking in tongues, interpreting tongues, prophesying, and teaching—all at the same time! Paul considered this situation to be in need of immediate correction, and in this portion of his letter he provides that correction.

Paul begins by contrasting the gift of prophecy with that of speaking in tongues (14:1-5). His point of contrast is that the public proclamation of prophecy can inspire the entire congregation, whereas the unintelligible sounds of speaking in tongues are only the private inspiration of the individual. While he does not want to eliminate the use of tongues, Paul does not hesitate to call prophecy the greater gift, basing his judgment on the principle that in the setting of worship the spiritual growth of the community should take precedence over that of the individual.

Paul continues to argue for the superiority of public over private spiritual gifts in the next section of this chapter (14:6-19). He proposes the example of speaking in tongues, then asks the rhetorical question of what good this gift is if it does not communicate something of benefit to the community (14:6). Just as music cannot communicate without melody, and foreign languages cannot communicate without meaning, a Christian cannot communicate without the use of articulate speech. This excludes speaking in tongues as an acceptable vehicle of communication (14:7-11). Again, Paul reminds the Corinthians that he bases his reasoning on the underlying principle of the good of the Church (14:12).

In the setting of public worship, interpretation is a necessary complementary gift to the gift of speaking in tongues, because interpretation makes intelligible what was unintelligible, makes public what was private (14:13). In the next few verses (14:14-17) Paul argues that prayer and praise are much more effective in the life of the community if there is a coherence in them between spirit and mind, so that they are not merely expressions of spirit. The mind, in other words, makes the spirit intelligible. It enables other Christians to affirm (to say "Amen" to) the content of one's prayer and praise. To dispel any possible assertions that he was putting down speaking in tongues because he himself had not been blessed with this gift, Paul boasts that he can outdo all of them when it comes to that, but that he would not think of using this gift in church, where it could serve no good purpose (14:18-19).

The gift of speaking in tongues had apparently become something of a stumbling block, somewhat akin to the "gift" of being able to eat meat which had been offered to idols. Those who had received the gift of being able to speak in tongues claimed spiritual superiority of a kind quite similar to the superiority of the "knowledgeable" in their eating of idol-meat. Paul calls for spiritual maturity in 14:20, implying that the fixation of certain of the Corinthians on the outwardly spectacular gifts, such as speaking in tongues, was the height of immaturity.

Hoping to demonstrate that speaking in tongues really wasn't the great gift it was held to be, he cites an incident in the Old Testament (Isaiah 28:11-13) in which God's people—who would not listen to the prophets, whom they could understand—are punished by being invaded and forced to listen to the incomprehensible muttering of their captors. Actually, he proves more than he wants to in 14:21-22, since his quotation considers foreign tongues as a judgment rather than a gift, and he isn't nearly as hostile to tongues as his use of this text would imply. This is a good example of Paul getting carried away and overstating his case! He returns to his real point in 14:23-25, where he reasons that visitors would be embarrassed if not scandalized by a church full of people speaking in tongues, whereas they would be challenged—perhaps even converted—by prophetic preaching, which they could understand.

Paul concludes this part of his letter by giving some specific instructions to govern the celebration of the Liturgy of the Word in Corinth (14:26-40). These particular instructions are dated. The general considerations on which they are based, however—". . . so long as everything is done with a constructive purpose" (14:26c), "make sure that everything is done properly and in order" (14:40), as well as the theological truth from which these considerations are derived, namely, "God is a God, not of confusion, but of peace" (14:33)—are universally valid.

It is interesting to note, in the context of these specific instructions, that Paul considered an individual's prophecy to be in need of confirmation by the community as a whole (14:29b). He sees no excuse for those whose prophecies carry them into frenzied behavior; true prophecy has its own built-in safeguards (14:32 33). Some scholars hold that his instructions to women (14:34-35) apply only to gossip (which is, of course, unChristian) and teaching (which was considered inappropriate for a woman to do at that time), since he does not criticize women who pray or prophesy in 11:5. Again, he is not in the least embarrassed to refer to Tradition (14:36) and to his own apostolic authority (14:37) as reason enough to obey his commands.

Question for Personal Reflection/Group Discussion:

1. Would you say that the Liturgy of the Word, as we experience it today, exhibits more or less life than it did in Paul's day? Why?

Chapter 20: The Resurrection: Central Event of Christianity

Please read I Corinthians 15. The climax of the whole long list of aberrations and abuses within the Corinthian church—more serious

even than sexual immorality, or eating meat which had been sacrificed to idols, or misunderstanding the true nature of the Eucharist—
more serious because its denial destroyed the very basis of Christian
faith—was the refusal on the part of some of the Corinthians to accept
the Resurrection. The Resurrection which this church, composed
largely of Greek converts, was rejecting was the specifically *bodily*
Resurrection of Jesus.

These former pagans had no problem with a nice "clean"
concept such as the immortality of the soul, but drew the line when it
came to raising up such a repulsive reality as the human body. In this
they were simply reflecting the body-soul dualism so prevalent in
Greek philosophy and culture. They thought they could be Christians
and just not accept this particular doctrine. Paul, of course, argues
otherwise. Chapter 15 is his extended discussion on the reality and
nature of the Resurrection.. In a way we are fortunate that some of the
Corinthian Christians doubted the Resurrection and that he responded
to them at length and in depth. Our understanding of this central
Christian reality would be immeasurably impoverished without I
Corinthians 15.

Paul begins by asking the Corinthians to remember the original
Gospel which he had shared with them (15:1). The quality of their
present response to the Gospel—a response which must include
fidelity to the content of that Gospel—is presently deciding their
salvation (15:2—notice the unusual use of the present tense in this
verse). He underscores the fact that the Gospel which he has
proclaimed to the Corinthians is the very same Gospel which was
given to him (15:3a). In other words, the message which he is about to
repeat is not some private revelation of his own, but the essence of the
apostolic Tradition.

He recites this Tradition in 15:3b-8. With the exceptions of 6b:
"most of whom are still alive, although some have fallen asleep" and
8: "Last of all he was seen by me, as one born out of the normal
course," which are personal additions, he is narrating an extremely
early profession of faith (indicated by the solemn introductory "that"

which opens each statement of faith: 15:3b, 4, 5).

This early creed emphasized the death, burial, and Resurrection of Christ (15:3b-4), and also cited witnesses to the Resurrection of Christ (15:5-8). Jesus' death is understood as an atonement for sin (15:3); "in accordance with the Scriptures" is almost certainly an allusion to the Suffering Servant of Isaiah 53. Jesus' burial is important (15:4) because it underlines the reality of his death and provides the basis for the claim of incorruptibility. The "in accordance with the Scriptures" of 15:4 alludes to Psalm 16:9-11, which the early Church interpreted as pointing to Jesus' Resurrection. The list of witnesses (15:5-8) consists solely of men, because only their testimony would be accepted in a Jewish court of law.

This citation of numerous witnesses (Jewish law required only two witnesses to be in agreement to substantiate a case) is fully intended to serve as proof for the reality of the Resurrection. Paul's mentioning that most of the five hundred are "still" alive" (15:6b) is an invitation to the Corinthians to ask them if they won't believe him. His substitution of "fallen asleep" for "dead" stresses his belief in the Resurrection. Christians who have died are really "asleep"; that is, waiting for Jesus to return, and with his return to bring them the gift of resurrection.

Paul gives his personal testimony to the reality of the Risen Lord in 15:8a, together with an expression of his wonderment at having been chosen to be an apostle (15:8b-9), and a brief defense of his ministry (15:10). He concludes this section by repeating what he had stated at the beginning: that this is official apostolic teaching (with the implication that they had better take heed!). Notice in 15:11 how he uses the *past* tense of believe. This suggests his disappointment at those who had previously accepted the fullness of the Gospel (including the bodily Resurrection), but who follow it no longer.

The entire tenor of this section betrays Paul's factual attitude toward the Resurrection. He—and apparently all the rest of the witnesses—does not consider the Resurrection to be a subjective or symbolic truth (as quite a number of contemporary theologians would have it) but the fundamental historical fact of Christianity. To be sure, this fact has given rise to both doctrine and theology. But for Paul the doctrine and theology of the Resurrection would be hopelessly counterfeit if this event had not really happened in history. For him and for the early Christians the Resurrection was the astonishing fact which made sense out of Jesus' life and death and which gave birth to the community of his disciples in the Church. Without the reality of the Resurrection there would have been no Church, no Christianity, no new saving relationship with God.

Paul meets the objection of his opponents head-on in 15:12. Apparently some of the Corinthians were willing to grant, by way of exception, a bodily resurrection for Christ, but not for anyone else. He uses simple logic to argue that if they deny the very possibility of resurrection, then Christ also has not been raised (15:13). Given the non-resurrection of Christ, certain things necessarily follow: the content of Christianity dissolves, and with it the possibility of faith (15:14). He returns to his legal imagery in 15:15 (another indication that his overriding intent is to establish a verdict solidly in favor of the Resurrection) and declares that if resurrection is an impossibility, he, and all true Christians, would be disclosed as "false witnesses," a crime punishable by death in Jewish law.

He repeats himself in 15:16-17, with the important addition in 15:17b that if Christ has not been raised, "You are still in your sins." In other words, Paul is establishing a connection between the Resurrection of Jesus and the forgiveness of sin. If the Father had not confirmed Jesus as Messiah, Lord, and Savior by raising him from the dead, his message—including his saving message of the Father's love, compassion, and forgiveness—would have been revealed as nothing more than another wild dream. Without the Father's life-giving testimony of the Resurrection, the Christian story would have been a particularly malicious form of fiction. Raising humanity to an unheard of intensity of hope, the death of its founder, when he had promised life, would have been an incredible letdown. Christians would have good reason to be the most bitter people on the face of the earth (15:19).

After this shattering account of faith without resurrection, Paul hastens to affirm the truth of the matter, which is that ''Christ is now raised from the dead'' (15:20). The notion of ''first fruits'' contains the promise of resurrection for all Christians. He has taken this Jewish ritual—offering the first part of a harvest to God in thanksgiving for the crop which will follow—and transposes the participants. Now it is God who offers the ''first fruits'' of Jesus' Resurrection to us as his pledge that all Christians will be raised in the same manner as his Son. Just as there is a real connection between the ''first fruits'' and the rest of the harvest, there is a connection between Christ and Christians, a connection which is real because of our mystical union with Christ through faith, Baptism, and the Eucharist.

Paul further develops the idea of solidarity with the Lord by contrasting the destructive connection between humanity and Adam and the redemptive connection between humanity and Christ (15:21-22). He fully accepts the Jewish understanding of a mystical solidarity between Adam and the rest of humankind; in a very real way all people share in the sinfulness of Adam. Through precisely the same kind of solidarity, however, all Christians share in the Resurrection of Christ; their death-dealing tie to sin has been overcome in the atoning death of the Lord; they are now able to receive the gift of resurrection life.

Paul soars into an eschatological vision (a vision of the last things) in 15:23-28. His vision encompasses a continuing war between good and evil. It is a war, however, in which the crucial battle has already been won through Jesus' Resurrection. The ''sovereignty, authority, and power'' mentioned in 15:24 refers to any forces which compete in any way with God. 15:25 alludes to Psalm 110:1, a psalm which he interprets as a messianic reference to Christ; 15:27 alludes to Psalm 8:7, another messianic interpretation. He takes care to exclude the Father from the subjection mentioned in 15:27b, because ultimately all will be subject to God (15:28). This subjection is an expression of worshipful relationship, not loss of identity.

The argumentative style of Paul is highly discursive; that is, he will pursue one line of thought to the end, then throw in new points as they occur to him. Writing letters, of course, encouraged this particular style. We can easily imagine St. Paul vigorously pacing up and down as he dictates a letter to his secretary—sometimes racing ahead so fast that the secretary has trouble keeping up, sometimes stopping to reemphasize something, often piling point upon point to forcefully state his case. I Corinthians 15 is a particularly good example of his discursive style in action. He heaps argument on top of argument to make his point. After all, his topic is the Resurrection, the central reality of Christianity, and he wants to be sure that he leaves no point unsaid, no base uncovered.

Following his mystical vision in 15:23-28, Paul returns to listing reasons why the Resurrection is a necessity. In 15:29 he refers to a curious practice in the early Church whereby Christians would receive baptism for the benefit of a dead non-Christian relative or friend, hoping that this baptism would somehow secure their salvation. He neither defends nor criticizes this practice; his point is that it is meaningless without Resurrection. Apparently some of the same people who were denying the Resurrection were also participating in this rite; he hopes to catch them in their own lack of logic.

It is interesting to note, in passing, that already at this early date Baptism was considered so essential and so effective for salvation that its effectiveness was held to extend even to those who had not been baptized in this life. This, of course, was taking sacramental theology too far; the fact that this excess occurred so early, however, points to a highly developed sacramental theology very early within the history of the Church.

Paul now speaks from personal experience, mentioning how he is constantly in danger for the sake of the Gospel, and how this danger would be pointless without the motivating power of the Resurrection to sustain him (15:30-32a). Incidentally, most commentators consider the ''beasts'' of 15:32a to be figurative, since Roman citizens, such as Paul, were not supposed to be subjected to this kind of punishment. However, there was an amphitheater in Ephesus in which gladiatorial combat was held, and we know both from his letters and from *The Acts of the Apostles* that a lot of things happened to Paul which were not supposed to happen.

If the Resurrection is not a reality, continues Paul, we might as well give up as Christians and start living according to the way of the world, taking our pleasure now, before we die (15:32b). It is significant that all major cultures of the ancient world, including Israel (as we know from Isaiah 22:13), had a saying to this effect. This kind of self-centered satisfaction was then—as it still is—the major alternative to a life of faith.

Paul abruptly turns from this materialistic dead-end and challenges the Corinthians to return to their senses (15:33-34). He quotes a Greek literary cliche, ''Bad company corrupts good morals,'' to the effect that the Corinthians had better part company with worldly unbelievers, since their lack of belief was beginning to rub off on them.

Up to this point Paul has been dealing with the fact of Jesus' Resurrection (15:1-11), and the implications of this fact, and its denial, for Christians (15:12-34). Now he responds to two inescapable questions, questions of curiosity which flow from belief in a bodily resurrection (15:35-49). Both questions are stated in 15:35: ''*How* are the dead to be raised up?'' and ''*What* kind of body will they have?'' He answers the first in 15:36-44a, the second in 15:44b-49.

The question of how the dead were to be resurrected was an impossible question for the Greek mind, rejecting as it did the goodness of the body. ''Good riddance!'' was the philosophical approach of the Greeks to bodily death. The soul was finally set free to pursue its quest for truth without the hindrance of the body. Indeed, to the Greek, one of the strongest arguments against bodily resurrection was the unavoidable fact that dead bodies corrupt and disintegrate; what would be left, then, to resurrect? Christian belief in bodily resurrection struck the Greeks as ludicrous. Concerning this aspect of Paul's preaching in Athens, *Acts* tell us that "When they heard about the raising of the dead, some sneered . . . " (Acts 17:32).

In the typical philosophical style of the day, Paul begins by turning the table on his opponents, asking them how they can ask such a stupid question (15:36a). He proceeds to argue from analogy. Just as there is continuity between a seed that is sown, undergoes "corruption," and "rises" to new life, so too, there is an essential continuity within the human body throughout its various stages: life, death, resurrection (15:36-37). God is perfectly capable of bringing life out of death, of creating a resurrection body from a body of death and decay (15:38).

Paul goes on to list all sorts of different types of bodies in 15:39-41. His point is that given the existence and the appropriateness of all these different kinds of bodies, who is to say that a resurrection body cannot exist or is inappropriate? Such narrow thinking is really an insult to the creative, life-giving intent of God! He wraps up his analogy in 15:42-44 with a series of four antitheses which are calculated to demonstrate God's awesome power in the Resurrection. The corruptible becomes incorruptible, the lowly glorious; weakness turns into strength, and the natural body is transformed into a spiritual body.

This reference to the "spiritual body" in 15:44 is, in effect, his answer to the second question: "*What* kind of body will they have?" To illustrate what he means by "spiritual body," Paul proposes another analogy (15:45-49). This analogy takes us back to the essential solidarity between humanity and Adam, Christians and Christ, which he has already introduced in 15:21-22. His point here is that there is a qualitative difference between the first Adam, who was a created being, and the last Adam (the Risen Lord) who is one with the Creator. Just as humankind shares in the limitations of the first Adam, limitations which lead to death, Christians share in the victory of the last Adam, a victory which includes the promise of the resurrected life of the "spiritual body."

For the Hebrews, as for Paul and the early Church, the dimension of the spirit included the dimension of bodily existence. Viewed from this perspective, resurrected life would not really be life unless it included a "spiritual body." The resurrected body is "spiritual" in the sense that it reflects the life of Father, Son, and Holy Spirit—it has transcended death and is no longer subject to earthly limitations; it is, nonetheless, a "body" in the sense that it embraces corporeality as an essential expression of personality. This notion of the "spiritual body"—an idea which is a contradiction in terms for the Greek—is one of the great affirmations of Christianity. It is, as Paul tells us at the beginning of this chapter (15:1-11), an affirmation based not just on theory, but on actual appearances of the Risen Lord. "We shall be like him" is the essence of his answer to both the *how* and the *what* of resurrection. "How are the dead to be raised up?"—They are to be raised up like him. "What kind of body will they have?—They will have a body like his.

In the final magnificent section of this magnificent chapter (15:50-58), Paul spotlights God's initiative and dominion throughout this whole resurrection process. He begins by baldly stating that human beings, in and of themselves, are totally powerless to effect their own salvation (15:50). The truth of the matter far surpasses anything that we could conceive or cause ourselves, and he has to take off on another mystical vision (15:51-55) to begin to describe the magnitude of what will happen. The heart of his vision is the fact that "all of us are to be changed" (15:51b). He has already gone into the how and the what of the change (15:35-49); here he simply affirms the reality of this change—in ourselves we are unfit for God's Kingdom; therefore, God will change us.

Using typical apocalyptic imagery—a visionary account of the "end"—Paul gives us a brief scenario of the last things, again highlighting the fact that "we shall be changed" (15:52). His own hope was that he would still be alive when Jesus returned, "Not all of us shall fall asleep" (15:51a). His attitude of hopeful anticipation should be as strong in us today as it was for him yesterday because God's promise remains the same. He repeats himself in 15:53-54a, gathering momentum to make his joyful shout in 15:54b-55: "Death is swallowed up in victory. O death, where is your victory? O death, where is your sting?" In this great victory-shout, he overcomes the tragic prophecy of Hosea 13:14 with the triumphant vision of Isaiah 25:6-8a.

In a parenthetical remark in 15:56, Paul, echoing the theology of Galatians, connects death, sin, and the law—the implication being that the law, in revealing God's will to us without empowering us to honor it, increased our sinfulness, ensnaring us more and more in death. But, he continues, this vicious circle has been broken forever in the absolute victory which the Father has given us in the life, death, and Resurrection of Jesus (15:57). Jesus, then, is the efficient cause of our own personal victory over death. Given such an incredible truth, such a staggering promise, how could our response be anything but to be "steadfast and persevering," dedicating ourselves more and more fully to the Lord's work (15:58)? Our life "in the Lord," his lifegiving relationship with us, empowers us for loving service in his name.

Reflection

I Corinthians 15 is undoubtedly one of the most inspiring passages in all of Scripture. It graces us with an in-depth development of the most central reality of our faith: the Resurrection of our Lord and Savior Jesus Christ. And yet a careful reading of this chapter cannot help but leave us with an unsettling question of our own, a question which Paul did not foresee when he authored this text. For Paul, Jesus' return was imminent, and with it resurrected life both for those Christians who had already "fallen asleep" and for those who were still alive at his Coming. The future tense which Paul uses throughout this chapter is a very *short* future tense. When Paul says

> . . . so in Christ all *will* come to life again (15:22b)
> . . . so *shall* we bear the likeness of the man from
> heaven (15:49b)
> . . . all of us *are to be* changed (15:51b)

the time span he envisions between present promise and future fulfillment is so short that he thinks that he will still be alive when Jesus
returns. Things did not work out that way.

Our problem—and a very personal problem it is, considering the
very personal relationship we share with the Lord—is: What is going
to happen to *us* between our deaths and the future Coming of the Lord
Jesus? Do we have to undergo the indefinite period of "sleep"
implied in this letter, having to wait, as it were, for the Lord's return
so that we can resume our relationship with him? Of course nothing
goes faster than a good night's sleep; still, this seems like a rather
empty substitute compared to the fullness of God's promise. What are
we to make of this dilemma?

One possible approach to this problem comes from St. Paul
himself. It seems that as he grew older—and it became more and more
apparent that perhaps Christ was not going to come back as quickly as
had been anticipated—Paul became more and more convinced of a
personal afterlife with the Lord which would precede one's bodily
resurrection at Jesus' return. Already in his second letter to the
Corinthians, Paul describes this pre-resurrection afterlife (II Cor
5:1-10).

This type of approach seems to square with the theology being
developed concurrently in the Gospels. In Luke, for example, Jesus
tells one of the criminals being crucified with him:

> I assure you: this day you will be with me in
> paradise. (Luke 23:43)

The most developed affirmation of an uninterrupted relationship with
the Lord comes in the Gospel of John. John presents salvation as a
present reality, not just a future hope. According to John, salvation

begins the moment one accepts a saving relationship with Jesus. In the Gospel of John, Jesus says

> Whoever has seen me has seen the Father (John 14:9).
> I am the resurrection and the life:
> whoever believes in me,
> though he should die, will come to life;
> and whoever is alive and believes in me
> will never die. (John 11:25-26).

Thus, what we find in the New Testament is a deepening insight into the mystery of what it means to live in relationship with Christ. At first, because Jesus was expected to return so soon, death was seen as a brief interruption of this relationship. As time elapsed it became clearer that one's relationship with Christ—because of the eternal nature of the primary partner—had to be something which was impervious to death. This insight is expressed most fully in the Gospel of John, where eternal life is seen as already present within one's present relationship with Christ.

Questions for Personal Reflection/Group Discussion:

1. Why is Jesus' Resurrection the single most important fact for Christianity?
2. Why do you think St. Paul presents his case for the reality of the Resurrection (15:1-11) in legal terms (terms which would be accepted in a Jewish court of law)?
3. What does the fact of Jesus' Resurrection mean to you personally?

Chapter 21:   Concluding Postcript

Please read I Corinthians 16. The contrast between this chapter, which is eminently practical, and the twin peaks of theology and mysticism expressed in chapter 15, can give us a telling insight into the nature of Christianity: it is a religion which concerns itself with *all* of life, and not just lofty principles. Thus, we find a creative counterpoint going on between Paul's glorious resurrection theology and the very down-to-earth business of this chapter.

The collection Paul refers to in 16:1 is an offering on the part of the Gentile churches to assist the mother church in Jerusalem, which was having a difficult time because of poverty and persecution. This collection will be a major topic in II Corinthians. "The first day of the week" in 16:2 is the earliest written evidence we have for Sunday being a special day of gathering for the Christian community.

Paul shares his travel plans with the Corinthians in 16:5-12. He hopes to spend a considerable length of time in Corinth; the extent and the depth of the problems beleaguering the church there would take some time to resolve. Perhaps Apollos declined to return to Corinth because he did not want to add fuel to the fire of factionalism.

Borrowing imagery from the military, Paul addresses a summary challenge to the Corinthian community (16:13). Being on "guard" highlights the fact that there were already things within the community which it was necessary to be on guard against. For Paul, to "stand firm in the faith" meant to remain faithful to the apostolic teaching in its original form; that is, as Paul himself had handed it to them. The key place given to love in 16:14 echoes Paul's words in I Corinthians 13; it is Paul's final reminder that love is primary. To "serve under such men" (16:16) implies that even at this early date distinctions were beginning to be made in the early Church in terms of authority. 16:19 witnesses to the fact that the early Christians did not meet in separate buildings, but in private homes. The "holy kiss" mentioned in 16:20 was soon to become a standard part of the liturgy, known today as the Kiss of Peace.

Paul personally writes his final remarks in 16:21-24. This was to authenticate the rest of the letter, which he had dictated to his secretary. It is interesting in 16:22b that Paul uses an Aramaic (a late form of biblical Hebrew, and Jesus' native tongue) phrase in an otherwise totally Greek letter. This phrase, *marana tha*, means simultaneously

"The Lord has come," "Our Lord is coming" and "O Lord, come!"
It was used as a kind of password/prayer among the early Christians, a
word by which they could recognize one another and gain access to
the often clandestine meetings of community worship. *Marana tha*
was, in itself, a short creed proclaiming faith in the Lord Jesus and
longing for his return. "Favor" in 16:23 is another word for grace.
Paul ends his letter on a note of love (16:24).

II Corinthians

Introduction

Paul's great pastoral letter (I Corinthians) did not improve the situation; apparently, it was rejected by a good part of the Corinthian community. This, of course, only made things worse. We can piece together the following sequence of events from a careful reading of II Corinthians: the hostile reception which his pastoral letter obtained sent Paul on a surprise visit. This visit was disastrous; not only was Paul unable to resolve the situation, someone —probably inspired by a group of false teachers who had made their way to Corinth—publicly insulted Paul. He left the city more personally injured than he had ever been before. Eventually he sent his trusted friend Titus back to Corinth with a passionately severe letter, hoping to win back the loyalty of this recalcitrant church.

This "severe" letter, referred to in II Corinthians, is another part of the Corinthian correspondence which we do not have—unless, as many scholars think, chapters 10-13 of our present II Corinthians are really part of this lost letter. They argue this on the basis of a marked change of style, and the fact that these chapters are, indeed, severe. However, anyone who has ever written a highly emotional letter, dropped it for a number of days, and then picked it up again, knows enough about the reality of changing content and style to grant this as the most plausible explanation of the "break" between chapters 1-9 and chapters 10-13.

At any rate, Paul did indeed send a severe letter to Corinth by way of Titus. He was so emotionally involved with its outcome, so troubled as to whether it would be accepted or rejected, that he abandoned a promising missionary opportunity where he was and rushed to Macedonia to intercept Titus and find out what had happened.

Titus brought good tidings. The Corinthians had punished the person who had held Paul in contempt and renewed their loyalty to Paul and the Gospel which he preached. Paul then wrote II Corinthians as a heartfelt response to the reconciliation which had occured. But there was more in his heart than simple reconciliation; he was still deeply hurt and could not help but go back into the areas of tension between himself and the Corinthians, tensions which he hoped to resolve definitively with this letter. Thus, Paul expends a great deal of energy in II Corinthians defending himself and his apostolate and putting down the false teachers who had incited the revolt against his authority. Add to this the fact that time constrained him to bring up the whole matter of a major collection for the benefit of the Jerusalem church, and one can begin to get an idea of the fragmented, even tumultuous, nature of this letter.

While there are several major divisions (falling along the lines mentioned above of Paul's vindication of his ministry, his refutation of his enemies, and the matter of the Jerusalem collection), there are so many digressions, breaks in thought, and repetitions in this letter that any attempt to neatly summarize its flow and contents could only mirror its underlying disunity. Better simply to enjoy it and learn from it as it stands—the most deeply personal and passionate letter that we have from Paul, full of insights into the meaning of faith and into the nature of his person.

Chapter 22:   Community as Communion of Saints

Please read II Corinthians 1:1-2:13. Following the typical letter-writing pattern of his day, Paul begins by naming himself (and Timothy, whom he probably mentions here to affirm the validity of his ministry, which may have been questioned), identifying the recipient, and giving a brief salutation. He is careful to acknowledge both Gentile Christians (''grace'' was a favorite Greek word of greeting) and Jewish Christians (who greeted one another with the word ''peace'').

The usual pattern would call for a thanksgiving at this point— every other letter except this one and Galatians has it. The fact that II Corinthians contains no specific ''thank you's,'' no personal words of appreciation for exemplary faith or works, is an early indication of Paul's disappointment and displeasure.

Instead of thanking the Corinthians, as would have been customary, Paul thanks God. 1:3-4 is a beautiful paean to the Father, expressing heartfelt thanks for his gift of consolation. The Greek word for consolation, or comfort, carries the positive connotation of enabling one to endure *with joy*. Thus, in thanking God for his consolation, he is not just thanking him for the strength to hang on, but for the endurance to hang on joyfully. These verses witness to the depth of Paul's personal relationship with the *Father*; his relationship with God, though centered in Christ, is also profoundly Trinitarian. It is noteworthy that immediately after thanking God for the grace of consolation in 1:3, he talks about how God's strengthening of him, in turn, enables him to strengthen others. Paul is here describing firsthand a crucial principle of Christian spirituality: namely, that God does not simply bless the Christian for the betterment of him—or herself; rather, he empowers the individual so that he or she may empower the community.

Paul goes on to expand his description of his experience of the Communion of Saints in 1:5-7. He boldly identifies his sufferings with those of Christ (1:5). In other words, the sufferings which he experiences as a Christian are the sufferings of the Lord himself. In a very real way Jesus suffers *with* the Christian, just as the Christian suffers *with* Jesus. United with the sufferings of Christ, our sufferings become, like his, redemptive. This is why he immediately expands the context to include the community, in this case the Christian community at Corinth.

Paul's sufferings, because they are connected with Christ's, have redemptive value for the Christian community as a whole. This same overflowing movement from the Father through Christ to the individual to the community is the way in which consolation (and, by extension, all other graces) is communicated. God's love is, fundamentally, a great process of sharing. God shares his consoling love with Paul who shares it with the Corinthians so that they, in turn, might share it with one another and offer it to the community at large. From a personal point of view, this whole section on the communion of saints (1:3-7) can be taken as a statement of Paul's solidarity with Christ and the community, and as his plea for their solidarity with him.

The near death experience which Paul refers to in 1:8-11 was apparently already known to the Corinthians who, however, did not fully grasp its seriousness. He turns it into a lesson of man's total dependence on God. This is the first instance of the contrast between human weakness and God's strength in this letter. It will become a major theme. Implied in 1:11 is the effectiveness of petitionary prayer. Petitionary prayer itself assumes the reality of the Communion of Saints.

Having prepared the way theologically, Paul goes on to defend himself personally. He begins his personal defense by tackling the charge of capriciousness. A likely reconstruction of events leading to this charge is that: (a) Paul announced that he would make another visit to Corinth on his way *from* Macedonia (I Cor 16:5-6); (b) a crisis occurred, necessitating his short surprise visit; either then, or shortly thereafter in his severe letter, he told the Corinthians that he would visit them *twice* more in short order; that is, both *to* and *from* Macedonia; (c) upon further prayerful consideration after his anger and anxiety had abated somewhat, he found his original plan (to pay them one visit, not two) to be the better one. His antagonists in Corinth jumped at the chance to point out his inconsistency; thus, the charge of capriciousness.

Paul launches his counterattack by insisting that his conscience is absolutely clear in regard to his conduct (1:12); so completely have his actions been rooted in his relationship with God that he can actually boast about his behavior. Boasting is a recurrent motif in his letters, especially this one. Christians tend to be disturbed by this trait of Paul's; they equate boasting with pride and consider it incompatible with humility. St. Paul would undoubtedly make a case for himself by calling attention to the fact that boasting, if done in the Lord—out of recognition of *his* power, not ours—can be a strong witness. Perhaps he would say that most Christians were too timid in their outward celebration of God's gifts to them. Timid, he definitely was not. True to character, he boldly extends his notion of boasting to express his hope that on the day of Jesus' return he (the Paul they now dislike so heartily) will actually be their boast, and they his (1:13b-14).

Paul reminds the Corinthians of his travel plans (1:15-16), asks two rhetorical questions in 1:17 (questions to which many of the Corinthians would have answered with a resounding affirmative), then presents the heart of his defense (1:18-22). He begins with a solemn oath, "As God keeps his word" (1:18a), testifying that what he has to say is "The truth and nothing but the truth." His declaration of innocence—that he is not guilty of breaking faith—follows, backed up by the strongest possible connection between his word and Christ's (1:19).

Paul is claiming that if Christ is faithful, so is he, because his actions—his outward expressions of faithfulness—flow from his relationship with Christ. As often happens with him, one inspired insight leads to another. Thus, the wonderful perception of Jesus being categorically "yes" prompts Paul to say something else about the nature of Christ; namely, that he is the Father's "Yes" to all the promises of the "old" covenant (1:20). In the person of Jesus salvation history has been completed; all we can do is to accept—to offer our own "yes" or "Amen" to—what God has already done for us in and through Christ.

True to form, Paul further expands his thought, climaxing in a mighty crescendo to Father, Son, and Spirit (1:21-22). These verses

are bathed in baptismal imagery: already in the early Church, Baptism
was understood as an anointing, or consecration, to the Father through
Christ; it was seen as sealing or confirming the baptized with the gift
of the Holy Spirit. Notice how in 1:21a, "God is the one who firmly
establishes *us along with you* in Christ," the reality of the communion
of saints is implied. Paul, in other words, continues to plead for
acceptance from the Corinthians.

The ancient custom of "first payment" was quite like our
practice of "down payment"—a guarantee that full payment would
be made. Paul is telling us that the undeniable presence of the Holy
Spirit in the life of a Christian is God's personal guarantee that full
payment will be made on the promise of our salvation in Christ. In the
immediate context of his confrontation with the Corinthians, he seems
to be claiming that the most telling proof that he is constant and not
capricious is that he—like them, if they are real Christians—is sharing
in the life of the Trinity (granted that "Trinity" was not yet doctrine,
the doctrine is certainly hinted at in 1:21-22).

Returning to his original subject (the charge of fickleness), Paul
swears another oath, "I call on God as my witness" (1:23), to prove
the sincerity of his motives. The reason he did not promptly return to
Corinth (as he had said he would) was that he feared another unpleas-
ant confrontation with them (1:24); their relationship was too precarious to risk another disastrous visit. Note Paul's praise in 1:24c.
Apparently his pastoral letter (I Cor) had helped to resolve some of
their questions of faith.

The next part of the letter (2:1-4) is a moving expression of
Paul's warm feelings toward the Corinthians. He had good reason to
be emotionally involved with them; after all, he was the founder of
their community, had lived among them for a considerable length of
time, had shared in their joys, sorrows, and struggles. The impression
we get of Paul in this section, and in many other places in this letter, is
that he was, first of all, a sensitive, flesh-and-blood human being; a
shepherd who loved his people and who was not afraid to show his
love.

Paul's passionate involvement with people goes counter to the notion of theology as an abstract, intellectual system. For him, Christian theology was the staff of life, which affected all areas of daily living. Just as the faith was worth fighting for (through intense missionary activity), it was also worth *feeling* for. Thus, Paul is not in the least ashamed to admit that he wept as he wrote his severe letter (2:4). He mirrored the intense relationality of God in his own intense relationships with his churches.

Paul's thoughts now turn to his last painful visit and to the person who had insulted or otherwise injured him (2:5-11). Again speaking from his underlying vision of the Communion of Saints, Paul gently reminds the Corinthians that the offender has wounded not only him, but the entire community (2:5). He does not dwell on the past, however. He acknowledges the fitness of the punishment (probably some form of excommunication), and asks that since it has served its purpose, it now be lifted (2:6-8). This is a good example of how ecclesiastical discipline was viewed by the early Church; it was seen to be for healing, not for destruction. Invoking yet again the reality of the Communion of Saints, Paul expresses his solidarity with the Corinthians (2:10). Just as injury affects the entire community, so too does forgiveness. In this way—through the healing, restorative power of Christian forgiveness—the designs of the devil (who would have liked nothing better than to have seen continuing hostilities within the community) are defeated (2:11).

Turning back to his description of his inner turmoil (2:12-13), Paul tells of a promising missionary opportunity which he had to abandon because he was too anxious about the response of the Corinthians to his letter. Titus had delivered the letter and was journeying back to Paul at Troas (on the northwestern coast of Asia Minor, near the site of ancient Troy) by way of Macedonia. Because of his anxious impatience, Paul drops everything and hastens to Macedonia to find Titus. We know from a later passage in this letter (7:5-7) that Paul did indeed find Titus and that Titus bore glad tidings. At this point, however, retelling his travels causes him to remember his mental anguish, and he goes off on a wild digression in defense of his ministry for several chapters in the biblical text.

Questions for Personal Reflection/Group Discussion:

1. Describe Paul's understanding of the Communion of Saints based on the hints contained in this section (II Cor 1-2:13).
2. Are you comfortable with the concept of "boasting in the Lord"? Why or why not?
3. How do you feel about Paul's transparency of feeling in this letter?
4. (a) Do you tend to be a "thinking" Christian or a "feeling" Christian, or both?
   (b) What does this tell you about your own spirituality?

Chapter 23:   Paul's Passionate Defense of His Ministry I: The Old Covenant Contrasted with the New; His Life as a Reflection of Christ's Life

Please read II Corinthians 2:14-4:18.   Paul begins with a prayer of praise (2:14). In the Greek the phrase "to God" stands first, emphasizing even more God's primary role in the ministry of salvation. He makes use of one of his favorite images, adopted from the practices of imperial Rome. It is that of the triumphal procession, in which a victorious Roman general would parade through the streets, showing off his army and his spoils of war, including prisoners on their way to execution. The procession would include incense-bearers, with their censers billowing clouds of fragrant smoke, reminding the general and his army of the sweet smell of victory, and giving the prisoners a bitter taste of defeat. Paul, of course, turns this pagan image into a Christian one. Christ becomes the victorious general, his apostles become the incense-bearers, and the Gospel becomes the incense (2:14).

The image expands in 2:15 to include the Old Testament understanding of sacrifice, in which God was believed to be pleased with the sweet-smelling smoke wafting up from the altar. Here the apostles themselves are likened to that fragrant smoke. In 2:15b-16 Paul divides people into two basic camps, depending on their self-chosen response to the apostles and their preaching of the Gospel. It truly becomes the Good News of life to those who accept it; those who reject it are really choosing a self-inflicted death over God's offer of life. The staggering nature of his mission—in which personal choices for life or death are being made every day—strikes Paul in 2:16b: "For such a mission as this, is anyone really qualified?" The answer to this rhetorical question is an obvious "No!" and puts the responsibility for empowerment where it should be: on God.

A sharp criticism of the false teachers who had arrived sometime after Paul's successful founding of the church in Corinth is contained in 2:17. They "trade on the word of God"; that is, one of the many ways in which their ministry is so unlike his is that they charge for their services, becoming rich by selling God's word. Their motives are deceptive. The motives of Paul, and all true ministers of the Gospel, are unequivocal because they flow from a true commission and a vital, ongoing relationship with God.

Paul indulges in some irony—if not sarcasm—in 3:1. Between the lines is the fact that the false teachers enjoyed bragging about themselves, even to the extent of getting others to brag for them in the form of letters of recommendation. He does not need such slick signs of approval; his letter of recommendation is the quality of faith, indeed, the very existence of faith in Corinth. His foundational role and their immense debt to him is something which the Corinthians know in their hearts. He does not dwell on his own part, however, but is quick to underline God's even more fundamental role in their conversion (3:3-6).

All he did was to deliver the letter (the Gospel message), a letter which was so wonderfully effective because it was not just another legal system (notice the reference to the Ten Commandments in 3:3c), but a living relationship with the living God. Paul bases his conviction of the worth of his ministry on the reality of this God-authored, God-given relationship, not on any particular talents of his own (3:4-6). He cannot help but contrast his new experience of sharing in a life-giving relationship with God with his "old" experience of trying to live according to the Jewish law. For him, "The written law kills, but the Spirit gives life" (3:6c).

Continuing his contrast between the old and new covenants (3:7-18), Paul goes into a lengthy, rather involved analogy based on Exodus 34:29-35. According to the Exodus account, Moses' face became radiant from being in God's presence. The Israelites, who associated this radiance with God's fearful holiness, were afraid of Moses, who took to covering his face with a veil so that he would not unduly disturb them. When Moses spoke with God, however, he would remove the veil. Paul uses this account as a springboard for a series of hostile contrasts between the old covenant and the new.

He begins by calling the old covenant a "ministry of death" (3:7a); this is so because the legal system of the old covenant revealed God's will in the form of commandments without, at the same time, providing the power to keep these commandments. Thus, the old covenant actually made things immeasurably harder for the person who wanted to follow God. Since it was impossible to successfully fulfill the law, the law led to death, not life. In spite of its bleak nature, however, the law was still somewhat glorious—glorious enough so that Moses' face was radiant when he received it. Paul uses this limited glory of the old covenant as the basis of his comparison. Given the fact that the law, grim as it is, is still glorious—how much more glorious is the new covenant, the "ministry of the Spirit" (3:8).

Paul continues the contrast in 3:9, this time describing the old order as the "covenant that condemned" and the new order as the "ministry that justifies." "Condemned" is another word for "death," because anyone guilty of disobeying the law was condemned to death; "justifies" is another word for "life," because anyone sharing in the "ministry of the Spirit" was justified by that Spirit—that is, empowered to stand in right relationship with God.

Seen from this point of view (the viewpoint of salvation), the new covenant so infinitely outshines and outlives the old that the old can be said to have ''passed away'' (3:10-11).

Paul claims authority on the basis of this new covenant (3:12). Again, he plunges into a hostile contrast, this time using the figure of the ''veil'' as his major point of contention (3:13-18). He interprets Moses' donning of the veil as a vain attempt to conceal his gradual loss of radiance from the people (3:13); to him the veil is a symbol of the incompleteness and transitoriness of the old covenant. In 3:14-16 he makes his metaphor more inclusive by applying it to the reading of Scripture (the Old Testament) at the Jewish synagogue service. According to him, the ''veil'' of incompleteness and transitoriness is present whenever the Scriptures are read outside of the new covenant; that is, apart from a Spirit-filled relationship with Christ as Messiah and Lord. To those who enter into such a relationship, the ''veil'' of misunderstanding is lifted and they are enabled to see the real meaning of Scripture. They are freed, in other words, from death to life, and this freedom is the gift of the Spirit (3:17).

In 3:17-18 Paul makes a bold equation between the Lord (the Risen Jesus) and the Spirit. We know from the many places in which he makes a clear distinction between Father, Son, and Spirit (see, for example, II Cor 1:21-22, 13:13) that he does not intend to assimilate them into one another. Rather, he is anticipating the Gospel of John (see John 16:5-16) in understanding the Holy Spirit as an extension of the Risen Lord; God's way, so to speak, of making it possible for Jesus to be personally present to many people at the same time. This whole section (3:7-18) comes to a grand climax in verse 18, where he draws together the themes of ''glory,'' ''veil,'' ''Lord,'' and ''Spirit.'' As Christians, we do not know our Lord through a veil; through the active presence of his Spirit in us, we know him face to face. This immediate knowledge—this intimate relationship—is empowering us to become more and more like him whom we know and love. We share in his glory; or, rather, he shares his glory with us.

Returning to a more specific defense of his ministry, Paul professes that his very calling is, in itself, a great act of God's mercy, or love (4:1); because his apostolate is founded on God's call, he refuses to become disheartened. And there was much that had happened in Corinth about which he might become disheartened. 4:2-3 detail some of the charges which the false teachers had levelled against him. They accused him of using devious methods (the Greek word for "shameful," "underhanded," and "cunning" [see II Cor 11:3] is the same one used to describe Satan's deception of Eve) and of distorting the Gospel. He repudiates these charges and appeals to the Corinthians to turn to their conscience for proof of his innocence. Adverting to his previous analogy of the "veil," he repeats that his preaching of the Gospel is opaque only to those who are rejecting it. The implication is that Paul's detractors, in rejecting him, have also rejected the Gospel.

Again anticipating the Gospel of John (whose "prince of this world" is equivalent to Paul's "god of the present age" [4:4]—see John 12:31, 14:30, 16:11) Paul sets the rejection of the Gospel squarely within the larger context of the ongoing struggle between God and Satan. This reference to the "god of the present age" is significant because it shows that St. Paul—unlike many contemporary theologians who consider it beneath them—took the devil seriously.

For the early Christians the power of Satan was not just a gratuitous theological construct, but a fact of their experience of life. Recognizing Satan's power ("naming" the demon, so to speak) was the first step to overcoming that power. Theologically speaking, the reality of Satan—an originally good being gone bad and now irrevocably opposed to God—is necessary for Christianity to avoid making evil a part of God (like most of the Eastern religions do). At any rate, Paul clearly saw life as a battlefield between good and evil, not as some evolutionary progression from good to better to best.

Paul takes the offensive in 4:5 and hurls his main charge against the false teachers who, as we know from elsewhere in this letter (see, for example, II Cor 11:5, 18) were preaching themselves instead of

Christ. Unlike these false teachers, who claim to be "superapostles" and demand all sorts of special privileges because of their exalted status, Paul sees his apostleship in terms of servanthood. He remains in a state of wonderment at God's choice of him to be an apostle; so awesome was his conversion experience that he compares it with God's original act of creation (4:6). Paul's whole ministry is really his personal "thank you" to God for his boundless grace in calling him to relationship.

Continuing to give God the glory, Paul purposefully contrasts his own weakness with God's strength (4:7). His purpose is to discriminate between the true source and impetus of ministry—God—and our own purely subordinate role in the matter. The thought of his own role being that of a totally dependent "earthen vessel" triggers in Paul a series of contrasts between his own powerlessness and God's power to rescue (4:7-8). Thus, he is "afflicted," but through God's power "not crushed"—that is, a way of escape is always opened for him; he is "full of doubts"—that is, totally baffled by the turn of events—but does not despair; he is "persecuted" but "never abandoned" by God; "struck down" by men, but through God's power "never destroyed"—not even death would be able to destroy him.

Paul now draws an amazing parallel between his own suffering for the sake of the Gospel and the suffering of Jesus himself (4:10-15). Indeed, because of his sharing in the complementary realities of the Mystical Body of Christ and the Communion of Saints, the parallel collapses and becomes an identification. Because he is a Christian—because he is empowered by Christ's spirit, receives Christ's Body and Blood; in short, because he lives out of a deeply personal relationship with Christ—in a very real sense his sufferings (and, by extension, the sufferings of *all* real Christians) are those of the Lord. In this way his sufferings become a revelation of Christ's presence in the world. Moreover, just as Jesus' sufferings were not pointless but redemptive, Paul's sufferings become redemptive in the light of his relationship with Jesus. Because of the intimate identification between Christ and the Christian, we believe that the Father, whose transforming love raised Jesus from the dead, will also raise us from the dead.

Paul's vision of Christian ministry (actually, we could just as easily say "Christian *life*" because for the Christian, ministry and life should be largely synonymous), then, is one of suffering servanthood. It is following in the footsteps of Jesus; indeed, allowing him to become present through our suffering. Thus he can say to the Corinthians "Death is at work in us, but life in you" (4:12) meaning, that he is, in effect, spending his life for them. Like Jesus, we Christians are ordained to offer the sacrifice of our suffering—and to trust that the Father will redeem it.

Still giving God the praise, Paul proclaims that his daily empowerment to live the strenuous life he does is itself a divine gift (4:16). Given God's promise of risen life with him—a promise he is already experiencing in a preliminary way through his present relationship with Christ—he does not consider his suffering to be burdensome (4:17). By keeping his sight on God's promise he is able to keep his suffering in perspective (4:18).

Questions for Personal Reflection/Group Discussion:

1. Theologically speaking, how is suffering meaningful for a Christian?
2. How might seeing your life as a reflection of Jesus' life help you to make more sense out of your personal suffering?

Chapter 24: Paul's Passionate Defense of His Ministry II: The Primacy of Reconciliation

Please read II Corinthians 5:1-7:16.   This long section deals mainly with reconciliation; however, there are some interesting digressions: 5:1-10 considers the interim period between death and resurrection;

6:14-18 warns against close ties with unbelievers—all this within the context of Paul's continuing defense of his ministry.

Paul's thoughts about the gradual deterioration of his body (4:16b) apparently triggered in him some further reflections concerning the meaning of death for the Christian. Also, given his recent near death experience at Ephesus (see 1:8-9), this topic was still very much on his mind. Perhaps it was the intensity of this recent encounter with death which prompted him to suspect that he might very well be dead when Jesus returned. He seems to be supposing this when he writes ''he who raised up the Lord Jesus *will raise us up* along with Jesus'' (4:14). This is quite a different stance from that assumed in I Corinthians 15:51, where he said ''Not all of us shall fall asleep,'' evidently including himself among those who were still to be alive when the Lord returned.

What we see happening here in a poignantly personal way to St. Paul is the dawning realization that Jesus might not return as soon as had been anticipated. He wrote I Corinthians 15 from the perspective of the *Parousia* (Jesus' return in glory), which he thought would happen in the *near* future. By the time he was writing II Corinthians, the combination of his own mortality plus the already serious delay in Jesus' coming, caused him to consider Jesus' return as something which would happen in the *indefinite* future.

In I Corinthians he had focused on the Resurrection because the resurrection of believers was an integral part of Jesus' return. In II Corinthians, with its elongation of time till the Second Coming, the question arises as to what is to happen to the believer in the interim period between death and eventual resurrection. Paul addresses himself to this question in 5:1-10. It has become a very personal question for him since he now senses that he himself will die before Jesus comes back.

Paul begins with a profound affirmation of faith (5:1). The difference between our present mortal body and our future imperishable body will be like the difference between a man-made tent and a temple designed and created by God. Then follows a moving description of the dilemma facing the Christian during the interim between Jesus' Resurrection and the Second Coming (5:2-5). Paul's way of expressing himself here seems strange and confusing to us, so we had best ascertain the context from which he speaks before proceeding.

For the Jew, to be separated from one's body meant spiritual as well as physical death. The Old Testament is riddled with references like the following:

> For among the dead no one remembers you;
> in the nether world who gives you thanks?
> (Psalm 16:6)

> Indeed, for any among the living there is hope;
> a live dog is better off than a dead lion. For
> the living know that they are to die, but the dead
> no longer know anything.
> (Ecclesiastes 9:4-5a)

> For it is not the nether world that gives you thanks,
> nor death that praises you; Neither do those who go down into
> the pit await your kindness.
> (Isaiah 38:18)

By the time of Jesus and Paul, a belief in an afterlife had developed within certain segments of Judaism (such as the Pharisees and the Essenes—the Dead Sea Scroll people). However, because of the fundamental unity in Jewish thought between the body and the soul, an afterlife could only be conceived of in bodily terms; thus, the Jewish idea of a *bodily* resurrection. The notion of a *bodiless* stage of existence was both foreign and frightening to the Jews.

Yet the reality of such a bodiless state was precisely the conclusion to which Paul was pushed. To be sure, he saw this only as an intermediate, or temporary, stage. It would be transcended at Jesus' return with the bodily resurrection. For those who died before the Second Coming, this bodiless existence was something which had to be endured till then. This does not sound very positive but, returning to our text (5:2-4), we can see that at this point in his development

Paul really was not very enthusiastic about the possibility. "We groan *while we are here*" (5:2a)—in other words, while we are still in our body; "even as we yearn to have our heavenly habitation envelop us" (5:2b)—in other words, while we hope that Jesus will return within our lifetime so that we can put on our resurrected body without having to take off our mortal one. "This it will, provided we are found clothed and not naked" (5:3). To be "clothed," in this type of metaphorical Jewish thinking, means to be alive; to be "naked" means to be dead—to have had to strip off one's body.

Thus, 5:3 could be paraphrased: We will receive our resurrected bodies if we are still alive at Jesus' return; if we have died, then we will have to face a bodiless, intermediate state of existence. The fact that Paul is still uneasy at the thought of this interim state becomes clear in 5:4, where he bluntly states that "we do not wish to be stripped naked"—that is, Paul does not want to die; he still hopes that he will be alive at Christ's return so that his present body will be transformed by his spiritual body ("so that what is mortal may be absorbed by life").

5:5 is a pivotal verse. It ends the preceding section (5:2-4) on a positive note of promise. Because of the guarantee of the Spirit, the Christian knows for a fact that resurrected life awaits him. This verse provides the foundation upon which Paul can build a moving expression of faith in 5:6-9).

So strong is Paul's faith in God's promise that in spite of his uneasiness at the idea of a bodiless intermediate state he does not lose heart. He realizes that now our life with the Lord is far from perfect (5:6), that we must largely be content to know God by faith rather than through direct experience. This echoes his insight in I Corinthians 13:12—"Now we see indistinctly, as in a mirror; then we shall see face to face. My knowledge is imperfect now; then I shall know even as I am known."

Even if death is only the door to bodiless existence and not immediately to resurrected life, still this bodiless existence is, at least in a preliminary way, being "at home with the Lord" (5:8b). Thus, death does not take us away from the Lord, but actually brings us closer to him. All that really matters is our relationship with Christ (5:9). From this perspective, death—and the interim state it ushers in—is not a bitter disappointment but another milestone on the way to the total fulfillment of resurrected life.

Paul returns briefly to his overall task of defending his ministry (5:11-13), before taking off on a magnificent description of the ministry of reconciliation. He testifies that his ministry flows from an attitude of respect and reverence (5:11a): he does not take his relationship with God for granted. Confident that God knows the sincerity of his motives and actions, he hopes that the Corinthians will also acknowledge his sincerity (5:11b). He refrains from writing his own letter of recommendation to them at this point (5:12a); the word "again" may refer to the "stern" letter in which he apparently did this. Ironically, Paul tells the Corinthians that this would be a perfect time for them to brag about him in response to the pretentiousness and insincerity of the false teachers. He defends his ecstatic experiences (which the false teachers were apparently questioning) on the ground that they are God-given, not self-induced (5:13); his *normal* self is dedicated to his ministry.

Paul deeds the motivation for his ministry to Christ (5:14a)—not an abstract Christ, but a person with whom he is in a love relationship. His ministry, in other words, is an expression of his personal relationship with Christ. Referring to Jesus' crucifixion in the latter part of 5:14, he centers on the solidarity of humankind in the saving death of Jesus. Jesus died (and was raised) "for all" (5:15a)—that is, for *every* person, regardless of age or sex or nationality; "so that those who live"—so that those who have accepted the life-giving gift of his death and Resurrection—might join with him in his ministry of reconciliation (5:15b).

Perhaps the false teachers had tried to rekindle the old fear of Paul's credibility as an apostle (see, for example, Acts 9:26-27) by reviving his pre-Christian history as a denier of Christ and a persecutor of Christians. He settles this account by testifying that "because of this" (a Greek phrase pointing back to what has gone before)—because of his faith in Jesus' redemptive death and Resurrection, because of his saving relationship with Christ—he no longer judges Christ (or anyone else, for that matter) according to pre-Christian criteria (5:16).

At this point he plunges into a profound description of the new life which he has experienced through Christ's ministry of reconciliation (5:17-21). This is the most powerful exposition of the meaning of reconciliation in the New Testament, receiving its power from the fact that it is Paul's personal witness and not just a conceptual statement.

Leading off with his favorite phrase "in Christ," his shorthand for a friendship with the Lord which is so intimate that it is transformative, Paul describes the nature of that transformation. The phrase he selects is "new creation" (5:17), a phrase which literally explodes with meaning. "Creation" echoes God's activity as set forth in the Genesis account. It is telling that in choosing his word for "new," Paul chooses the word which means something new not just in time, but in *quality*. The creation brought about by being "In Christ" is a creation which is qualitatively new, radically different from anything which has preceded it. Written between the lines of this verse is his conviction that Jesus' life, death, and Resurrection mark the dividing line between two fundamentally different periods of human history. Everything before Christ is part of the "old order." Those who accept the gift of friendship "in Christ" become part of the "new creation."

This whole process of re-creation has been initiated and effected by God, who re-creates by reconciling us to himself through the unconditional and sacrificial love of Christ (5:18-19). Significantly, Paul uses the word "reconciliation," with its relational overtones, instead of the word "justification," with its legal, and often legalistic, undertones. "Reconciliation" is a more personal and personable word than "justification". By using it, Paul spotlights the relational nature of God's "new creation." Not only does living "in Christ" gift us with a new relationship with God, it give us a share in Jesus' ministry. Through Jesus, our reconciled relationship with the Father overflows into a ministry of reconciliation which reaches out to others, inviting them to share in God's "new creation." The Christian thus becomes an "ambassador for Christ" (5:20a), a "sacrament" person who is charged with the task of making Jesus present to others.

Paul wastes no time in using his ambassadorial role to present the Corinthians with a solemn call to reconciliation (5:20b). While this call is expressed in terms of reconciliation to God, because of the solidarity of Christians with one another through their solidarity with Christ, it contains an implicit appeal for reconciliation with himself as well.

5:21 summarizes what went before, and also briefly considers the "how" of reconciliation. In the original Greek text the phrase "him who did not know sin" stands first, emphasizing Jesus' sinlessness. The word used for "know" stands for personal (as opposed to abstract) knowledge, again stressing Jesus' purity. Considering his recent accent on the sacrificial death of Jesus in 5:14-15, Paul's cryptic statement about God making "him who did not know sin to be sin" is probably intended to spotlight the efficacious nature of Jesus' sacrifice. This, of course, evokes the rich sacrificial imagery of the Suffering Servant of Isaiah 53, and the sacrificial nature of the Eucharist.

Given the strategic placement of this verse as the climax to his section on reconciliation, we can safely say that Paul sees the Father's acceptance of Jesus' sacrifice as relational, not juridical. In other words, the Father accepted Jesus' death because it was the ultimate act of *love*, not because it was an adequate ransom, or punishment, for sin. Indeed, the unconditional and sacrificial love which brought about Jesus' death should not be confined just to Jesus, but extended to the Father (and, by implication, to the Spirit). "For our sakes *God* made him . . ." means that Jesus' sacrificial death was a great act of love on the part of the Father. In this relational context, II Corinthians 5:21 reads amazingly like John 3:16:

Yes, God so loved the world
that he gave his only Son,

that whoever believes in him may not die
but may have eternal life.

Given the impassioned nature of this letter, it is not surprising that Paul should occasionally exhort the recipients to the same depth and quality of faith that he has himself. He does just this in 6:1-2. The plea "not to receive the grace of God in vain" (6:1) assumes that it is indeed possible to abandon one's faith, and thus to reject the gift of salvation. Paul quotes from the prophet Isaiah in 6:2, transforming a past communication into a present challenge. He wants an immediate response on the part of the Corinthians, and he wants this response to include a complete reconciliation with God and with himself (see 5:20).

After this apostolic exhortation, Paul returns to his defense of his ministry (6:3-10), then renews his appeal to the Corinthians to become reconciled with him (6:11-13).

Paul states how careful he has been not to give anyone any reasons for criticizing him or his ministry (6:3). Instead, he does everything possible to make certain that his ministry is exemplary (6:4a). To confirm the authenticity of this statement, he offers a detailed listing of his qualifications (6:4b-7), beginning with the foremost, which is "patient endurance," the God-given ability to transform afflictions into blessings. He lists some of the afflictions which he has had to overcome. They include "natural" hardships (the inevitable struggles of living in this world)—"trials," "difficulties," and "distresses" hardships inflicted on him by hostile people—"beatings," "imprisonments," and "riots" hardships which he has had to inflict on himself—"hard work, "sleepless nights," and "fastings."

Returning to his list of qualifications (6:6), Paul mentions "innocence"—integrity, guilelessness; "knowledge"—his personal understanding of the Gospel, which spills over into his attitudes and actions; "patience"—forebearance with the shortcomings of others. These qualities are not his own achievements, but evidence of the presence of the Holy Spirit in his life; they are expressions of *agapé*, that uniquely Christian form of unconditional and abiding love.

Paul goes on to underline the truth and the power of the Gospel which he preaches (6:7a). His Gospel is powerful because it it true, true because it is the Word of God. All these attributes he uses as "weapons of righteousness" (6:7b), both offensively ("right hand") and defensively ("left") as the need arises.

At this point Paul becomes very personal and cites nine pairs of contrasts (6:8-10), each of which he has experienced intensely. Each contrast consists of a negative accusation, event, or reality followed by its positive counterpart. His point in offering these antitheses is that in spite of all opposition—including, by implication, the opposition of the false teachers at Corinth—his ministry has triumphed. He hopes that the passionate outpouring of his heart—here and throughout the rest of this letter—will encourage the Corinthians to respond to him in kind, thus effecting a complete reconciliation between themselves and their spiritual father (6:11-13).

The next section, 6:14-7:1, is considered by many scholars to be out of place here, since it changes the course of discussion so abruptly. They regard it as part of the early lost letter which Paul mentions in I Corinthians 5:9—"I wrote you in my letter not to associate with immoral persons." It fits this description well. However, as we have already seen on not a few occasions, sudden turnabouts in content and mood are certainly not unusual for Paul. We can easily imagine him fervently appealing to the Corinthians, remembering one of his strongest complaints against them—their all-too-easy associations with non-Christians—and indulging in some rather strong instruction before returning to his pleas for reconciliation. Perhaps he has just learned that some of the Corinthians who considered themselves "knowledgeable" were still taking part in pagan sacrifices—this would have been sure to ignite his censure! At any rate, it is probably more judicious to let the text stand as is rather than to postulate an unnecessary theory.

Paul introduces his topic in the strongest possible way (a way sure to inspire the ire of those in Corinth who, indeed, had formed close alliances with non-Christians) by using the verb meaning "to hitch together different species of animals" to describe the anomaly of close unions between Christians and unbelievers (6:14a). The Greek verb brings to mind (as he had undoubtedly intended it to) the Old Testament injunctions "You shall not plow with an ox and an ass harnessed together" (Deuteronomy 22:10) and "Do not breed any of your domestic animals with others of a different species" (Leviticus 19:19a).

To further hammer away at his point, Paul now makes five pointed antitheses contrasting Christians with unbelievers (6:14b-16a). The positive sides of the antitheses, "righteousness," "light," "Christ," "believer," and "temple of God" (in the *New American Bible* translation) are all aspects of Christian community. The negative sides, "lawlessness," "darkness," "Belial" (an obscure reference to Satan), "unbeliever," and "idols," call attention to the dangers involved in close associations with pagans. The last antithesis, the contrast between the "temple of God" and "idols," is particularly forceful, since it pits "the living God," who is present within the Christian community, against idols, which are dead and meaningless, but nevertheless demonic.

Paul concludes this digression (6:16b-18) with a pastiche of Old Testament quotations (a collage from Leviticus, Ezekiel, Isaiah, Jeremiah, and II Samuel)—all of which promise God's presence among his people, a holy presence which requires them to remove themselves from all vital contacts with unbelievers. Given these promises, the only adequate response is a really thoroughgoing conversion—a conversion of the total person, including both bodily and spiritual dimensions—on the part of those who consider themselves to be Christians (7:1).

His instruction completed, Paul resumes his passionate plea for reconciliation (7:2-4). Apparently still somewhat on the defensive because of the criticisms which have been aimed against him, probably most forcefully by the false teachers who have invaded Corinth, he continues to defend his ministry in the strongest possible terms (notice the threefold "no one" in 7:2b, which highlights his innocence). Reiterating his love for them, he reminds the Corinthians that they are indissolubly linked together, even to the point of being bound up in a common death and resurrection (7:3). Savoring again his happiness at the good news he has recently received from Titus, he reassures the Corinthians of his unlimited good will towards them (7:4).

At this point (7:5-16) Paul returns to his description of the emotions and events surrounding his reunion with Titus, a description begun in 2:12-14, but then broken off till now. He is quite candid (an indication of the deeply personal nature of his relationship with the Corinthians) in his sharing of the extreme turmoil he was in before finding Titus, and the intense joy he experienced with the coming of Titus and the favorable news from Corinth (7:5-7). He had had some doubts about the prudence of sending the severe letter; he risked straining his already strained relations with the Corinthians even further. Yet he sensed that it was only through a total and totally passionate confrontation that the crisis could be exposed and overcome.

Paul was right, and he expresses his simultaneous sadness and joy—sadness at having had to push things to the point of confrontation, joy at their complete turnabout as a result of it (7:8-9). In a brief theological interlude (7:10), he points out the crucial difference between sorrow which is offered to God and thus transformed into various life-giving spiritual gifts, and sorrow which focuses on itself, becomes bitter, and eventually destroys the person. He enumerates some of the blessings which the Corinthians have already received through their Godly sorrow (7:11), again rejoices at the good outcome of the letter (7:12), and enthusiastically shares with them his delight at Titus' delight with the happy outcome of his journey (7:13-16).

Questions for Personal Reflection/Group Discussion:

1. Describe the doctrine of reconciliation according to St. Paul.

2. What specific things about your life witness to the reality that through your relationship with Christ you have become a "new creation"?

Chapter 25: Christian Generosity

Please read II Corinthians 8-9. Having celebrated his growing reconciliation with the Corinthians, Paul feels his relationship with them secure enough to bring up the rather delicate subject of the collection for Jerusalem. This was no new topic; he had mentioned it in passing at the end of his pastoral letter (I Cor 16:1-4). Probably what had happened is that they had begun the process of saving for the collection, only to let it fall by the wayside when their conflict with him intensified. He now tactfully (and sometimes, as is his way, not so tactfully!) reminds them of their commitment in the next two chapters (8 & 9) of the present letter.

He begins by bringing to their attention the formidable example of the overwhelming generosity of the Macedonians (8:1-8). Corinth, which was the capital of Greece at that time, viewed Macedonia much as Jerusalem regarded Galilee: uncultured, backward, rather poor, and quite a bit behind the times. Thus, between the lines of his effusive praise of the Macedonians is the subtle pressure that of course the Corinthians—who were, comparatively speaking, much wealthier—would not want to be shown up by the Macedonians. Indeed, Paul goes so far as to present sharing in the collection as a "favor," or "grace," the grace of being able to participate in an act of loving concern, which is good psychology as well as good theology (8:4). He reminds them of Titus' past efforts concerning the collection (8:5), lists several of the areas in which they are particularly strong as a community (8:7a), and expresses his hope that they will also be strong in the area of giving (8:7b).

Paul now heightens his appeal by drawing a parallel between the sacrificial giving which he is asking them to do, and the ultimate act of sacrificial giving which Christ already accomplished (8:9). In the Greek the phrase "for your sake" begins the sentence to emphasize the immeasurable benefits which the Corinthians have already received, the clear implication being that the magnitude of Jesus' sacrifice should inspire them to give generously. This verse (8:9) is a beautiful statement of the mystery of the Incarnation. It assumes Christ's pre-existence (a significant theological fact considering the early date of this letter) and is a sort of shorthand version of Philippians 2:5-11.

Paul's advice on giving (8:10-15) is based on the principle of equality. It was obvious to him and the other apostles that a reality such as the Communion of Saints was not just a *promised* reality (that is, something which would be experienced in heaven), but also a *present* reality. It was something quite capable—through God's grace—of being incarnated in the here and now, at least in a preliminary way. And to the early apostles, part of embodying the Communion of Saints in the present meant that all who belonged to this Communion should experience a certain parity of material goods (see, for example, Acts 2:44-45). Thus, it was only a matter of course that richer Christians should substantially help poorer ones. To underline this basic principle of applied theology, Paul quotes Exodus 16:18 (in II Cor 8:15). The context is that of the gathering of the manna during the Israelites' desert experience. The point is that just as God would not countenance any gross inequality in the amount of manna which any individual or family took in, so also Christians (who are, after all, the Body of Christ in this world) should not tolerate any major disproportions as far as material needs are concerned.

In the next section (8:16-24), Paul reports on the latest developments concerning the collection. Titus has left for Corinth; with him are two others (apparently already well-known to the Corinthians, since Paul describes them without giving their names), who will help Titus with the work of the collection. He is careful to point out how he has sent delegates (8:20-21); by not directly involving himself he hopes to undercut any allegations which his enemies might make about his profiting from the proceeds. Thus, this section conveys yet another expression of his irreproachable conduct in connection with his ministry, and also serves as a letter of recommendation for Titus and his helpers.

Scholars who jump at the chance to divide and conquer the biblical text consider chapter 9—because of its slight repetition in content of chapter 8—to be part of another letter. This letter, it is hypothesized, was tacked on to 8 because of its similarity in content. A simpler, more likely explanation is that Paul, after a break in dictation, picked up where he left off (probably without reviewing what he had written previously), this time approaching the collection from a different angle.

Paul's angle of attack in the first part of this chapter (9:1-5) is somewhat humorous, uncovering as it does the fact that he had also been bragging to the Macedonians about the generosity and readiness of the Corinthians (just as he had been bragging to the Corinthians about the Macedonians in 8:1-5!) as part of his campaign to get them to respond with liberality. He is about to leave for Corinth in the company of some Macedonians, and is concerned that the collection at Corinth indeed be ready, so that no one will be embarrassed.

Returning to theology, Paul states a basic principle in 9:6; namely that the stingy person will receive few blessings, while the generous person will receive many. Underlying this statement is the truth that like begets like. On a deeper level, giving generously—taking a risk for God, so to speak—makes a person more dependent on God, thus giving God more room to work in his or her life.

What often happens is that the truly generous person receives an abundance of spiritual gifts, gifts whose nature it is to overflow into yet more bountiful giving (9:7-11). Paul concludes his discussion of the collection by pointing out the significant element of praise and thanksgiving which this act of generosity will inspire in those who receive it (9:12-15). The predominately Jewish Christian church of Jerusalem and the predominately Gentile churches of Greece cannot help but be drawn closer together by this act of goodwill.

Questions for Personal Reflection/Group Discussion:

1. What do you think Paul would have to say concerning the level of material equality of Christians throughout the world today?
2. (a) Do you think Paul would be pleased or displeased with the general level of giving in your parish? Why?
   (b) Do you think Paul would be pleased or displeased with your personal level of giving? Why?
3. Have you ever experienced blessings flowing from sacrificial giving? Please describe.

**Chapter 26:   Paul's Passionate Defense
of His Ministry III: Climactic Confrontation
with the False Teachers**

Please read II Corinthians 10-13.   Chapters 10-13 comprise another of those sections which many scholars believe to be out of place and originally part of a different letter. There is much evidence for this being the case with this particular section: in 10-13 reconciliation seems not to have happened yet, whereas in 1-7 it seems to be more or less assumed; a number of words, such as "to boast," which Paul uses in a positive, friendly way in 1-7, become negative and belligerent in 10-13. It could well be that this section is part of the sad and severe letter which Paul mentions in 2:4 and 7:8. Still, it is possible to account for the change of tone by a rather prolonged break in dictation, and to explain the hostility by seeing it as directed, not to the main body of the Corinthians with whom he is well on the way of reconciliation, but at the false teachers and those who sided or are still siding with them. These four chapters are the most passionately personal of any in his letters. They reveal to us a Paul who, just like the rest of us, very much needed to be loved and accepted—even celebrated—by those whom he was serving.

The way in which Paul begins (10:1a) is an indication of what is to follow. Much of what has preceded in this letter has been stated in fairly unemotional "we" form; here (in chapters 10-13), however, he speaks largely in an agitated first person singular. His reference to the "meekness" and "kindness" of Christ could almost be seen as ironic, considering the vehemence of what is to follow. More likely, though, they express his commitment to these Christian ideals—ideals, which, in the present context, he himself is not able to follow. Already in 1:1b he hurls back one of the charges made against him—that he makes up in his letters what he lacks in his person—a charge which obviously deeply hurt him, and to which he will return in 10:10.

Paul's "begging" in 10:2 is really a reluctant threat to the effect that when he returns he will not hesitate to use his apostolic authority to punish any remaining opposition. He underlines the God-given nature of his authority in 10:3-8, repeating his threat of punishment. The unmistakable implication in these verses is that since his message and authority come from God, to oppose him is to oppose God. We can sense something of the internal struggle which he is experiencing when he clearly states in 10:8 that his authority as an apostle is for "upbuilding," not "destruction." Concurrently, he angrily remembers the taunt about the strength of his letters and the weakness in his person (10:9-10), and repeats his threat of punishment a third time (10:11).

The depth to which Paul has been hurt can be seen in the supremely sarcastic way in which he begins the next section (10:12-18). The "certain people who recommend themselves" (10:12a) are the false teachers who had largely usurped his rightful authority and influence. He accuses them of writing extravagant letters of recommendation for themselves (10:12b), recommendations which are obviously false since they are self-given, not God-given, like Paul's (10:13).

The Greek word for "mark" in 10:13 is the word from which we get our word "canon," in biblical studies signifying the official measure (or listing) as to which books "belong" to Holy Scripture. In Paul's context, he means that he has remained within the bounds of his calling, whereas the false teachers have grossly overreached theirs. They have done this not only by taking over a mission which was his (10:16b), but—to add insult to injury—also by claiming as theirs work which he had already accomplished (10:15a). Given his anger, 10:17 stands as a prophetic denunciation of these false teachers, reminiscent of Jeremiah 9:22-23. Verse 18 clearly implies that Paul believes that God will vindicate his ministry, while disclaiming that of the false teachers.

Conscious that his impassioned outbursts are likely to be embarrassing for the Corinthians as well as for himself (11:1), Paul asks their forbearance for what is to follow. He compares his ardent concern for their loyalty and well-being to God's jealousy for his people in the Old Testament (11:2a), and draws an analogy between his role in the community and the betrothal customs of the time (11:2b). These customs held that the father was responsible for the purity of the bride until the engagement was consummated in marriage. Thus, as their spiritual father, Paul considers himself responsible for their spiritual purity until the consummation of their relationship with Christ upon his Return.

Paul takes his responsibility very seriously, and angrily states his anxiety that in the same way that Eve was lured away from the truth by the wiles of Satan, the Corinthians are on the verge of giving in to the counterfeit teachings of the false apostles (11:3). He has good grounds for expressing his concern, given the hearty welcome and enthusiastic response they have already given these false teachers (11:4). His threefold contrast, "another Jesus than the one we preached," "a different spirit than the one you have received," and "a gospel other than the gospel you accepted" emphasizes the weightiness of their near defection and the keenness of his anger.

Turning once more to self-defense (11:5), Paul testifies that as an apostle he is second to none (11:5). Note his sarcasm in naming his enemies "super-apostles." He admits that in speaking ability he may be deficient, but that (unlike his detractors) he is a faithful communicator of the true Gospel (11:6).

Of all the charges against him, probably the one which irritated him the most was the false accusation that he could not be a real apostle because he would not accept payment for his services. His enemies made this out to be a self-indictment by saying that this was his tacit way of admitting that his Gospel and his apostleship were second-rate. This type of malicious reasoning particularly infuriated him because it turned the truth into its opposite. Thus the vehemence of his defense and counterattack in 11:7-15.

Paul begins this section by asking a bitterly rhetorical question in 11:7—was it so terribly bad of him to have offered the Gospel to them without any financial strings attached, especially when he did this so that they might be able to accept it all the easier? He purposely exaggerates in 11:8 by using the phrase "robbed other churches" to describe how he had maintained himself during that time (supplementing his modest income as a tentmaker); ironically, the churches supporting him were the "poor" churches of Macedonia (11:9)!

Paul is justly proud of the fact that he has been able to offer the Gospel to them free of charge, and vows in the strongest possible terms (in the name of Christ) that he will never cease to do so (11:10). He makes it clear that this is not to spite the Corinthians—many of whom would have sincerely liked to have seen him paid for his services in Corinth out of Corinthian funds—but to defy the false apostles, who would have immediately used his fee to justify their own, and to claim equality with him on this basis (11:11-12). Switching from the defensive to the offensive in 11:13-15, he fiercely turns on his enemies by naming them "false apostles," linking their ministry to Satan and predicting their dire end.

In the next major section, 11:16-12:4, Paul decides to beat the false apostles at their own game of boasting. If they have impressive credentials in terms of background, so does he (11:22). Their sufferings cannot possibly compare with his incredible litany of sufferings (11:23-33). And in the realm of mystical experience, he again reigns supreme (12:1-4).

Paul realizes that this whole attempt to confirm his superiority is supremely foolish (11:16-17; 23b); yet he is constrained to "prove" himself in this way simply to disprove the claims of the false apostles (11:18). He is indignant that he has been forced to use these low tactics; yet, considering the fatuousness of his audience (the Corinthians!) in so warmly receiving the claims of the "super-apostles," perhaps they will take him more seriously now that he has stooped to speak on their level (11:19-21). This is Paul's sarcasm at its most biting; his fury comes through loud and clear.

Apparently part of the false teachers' claim to fame as "super-apostles" was their incomparable Jewish pedigree (11:22). They were "Hebrews"—that is, they prided themselves on still being able to use their native tongue; "Israelites"—they continued to practice the rigorous religious traditions of Judaism; "seed of Abraham"— through purity of lineage they claimed to be the inheritors of God's special promises to Abraham. This parade of prerogatives certainly would have been impressive to many of the Gentiles in a predominately Gentile church (the Jewish Christians probably would have felt somewhat put down by these claims, since many of them were not nearly as "pure" as their Palestinian counterparts). Paul emphasizes that he too enjoys all of these qualifications. So far, then, the "race" between him and the false apostles is neck-to-neck.

Paul pulls ahead dramatically by detailing his sufferings in 11:23-33. Again, he realizes that what he is trying to do—to "prove" his superiority in this way—is the height of foolishness (11:23a); but he is so upset that he does it anyway. And one must admit that his list of sufferings for the sake of the Gospel probably has not been surpassed in the entire history of Christianity. His suffering was not only physical, but mental; he constantly worried about the well-being of the churches he had founded (11:28-29).

Paul seems to have reached a watershed in 11:30; he has spent himself and realizes that the only thing that really matters in all this bragging is his weakness, because it is precisely his weakness—his vulnerability—which gives God the room to operate in his life. Remembering this, he mentions a specific instance of his weakness (emphasizing its truthfulness by relating it under oath), the occasion when he had to be smuggled out of Damascus in a basket (11:31-33). This must have been a continual source of embarrassment to him since he offers it as a paramount sign of his weakness.

If Paul had dramatically pulled ahead of the competition with his recital of sufferings, he now leaves them in the dust by brandishing his "final" commendation, his mystical experience (12:1-4). Again, Paul expresses embarrassment at having to use the coarse tactic of boasting (12:1); again, he proceeds full steam ahead. He relates his experience (12:2-4) in the third person to emphasize that the vision was from God, not something of his own doing; also, it makes him appear a bit more modest! The experience was so intense that he does not know "whether he was in or outside his body" (12:2b,3); that is, he does not know if he participated in this experience in a bodily way, or if his body was left behind in an out-of-the-body experience. The term "third heaven" (12:2c) is a Jewish phrase designating "highest" heaven, the closest possible encounter with God. The experience of revelation given to Paul was so transcendent, so holy, that to share it would be to desecrate it (12:4).

Paul considers the remarkable nature of this vision to be just cause for boasting—boasting, he realizes, of God's extraordinary gifts, not his own accomplishments (12:5a). The only thing that he could boast about in his own right would be his "weakness" (12:5b); that is, the exceptional ways in which he has allowed God to minister through him. Of course, even these "weaknesses" would eventually have to be traced to God's grace. At any rate, he resists the temptation to say more than he should about his vision. He does not really want people to base their estimate of him on the quality of an isolated mystical experience, but on the quality of his life and ministry as a whole (12:7a).

His mention of "weakness" above (12:5b), incites him to dive into this topic more deeply—and more personally (12:7b-10). He frankly admits that he does have a tendency toward pride (12:7b), a tendency which his extraordinary mystical experience could easily have fanned into extreme conceit. To counteract this penchant for vainglory, he interprets a particularly embarrassing personal imperfection (either a recurrent disease or a physical handicap of some sort) as God's way of keeping him humble (12:7c). Paul had struggled mightily with this debility, repeatedly imploring God to heal him (12:8; in this context "three" probably means "often"). The lesson he learned from God's refusal to do what he wanted was a hard but profound one (12:9): he learned that it was precisely through his weakness—that part of himself which he would most have liked to leave behind—that God could work most powerfully.

This is one of the great paradoxes of the Christian life. The fact that Paul was able to surrender to this truth (he speaks of his petitions and God's response in the *past* tense) demonstrates that he really was Christ-centered, not self-centered. He states specifically that he is able to endure not only his physical infirmity, but all his other sufferings, "for the sake of Christ" (12:10). He has learned the weighty lesson of letting *God* transform his weakness into strength. In this way his ministry is a constant witness to God's power to bring life out of death.

At this point, after all this relentless boasting, Paul catches his breath—"What a fool I have become!" (12:11a)—before careening on in his defense. He tries to turn the tables on the Corinthians by pointing out that his boasting would have been unnecessary if they had defended him as they should have and done his boasting for him (12:11b). He reminds them of his mighty works among them, works which authenticate his apostleship (12:12). He summarizes them under the traditional tripartite division of "signs"—actions which are symbolic of God's presence; "wonders"—unusual occurrences (such as healings or exorcisms) which by their very unusualness point to God; and "deeds of power"—impressive feats in which God can be seen to be directly at work.

The only way that Paul has treated the church at Corinth differently than he treated some (but not all) of his other churches was that at Corinth he refused payment for his services (12:13). His sarcastic remark "Forgive me this injustice!" is filled with exasperation. "One would have thought," he seems to be saying, "that you would have found this arrangement to your liking. Instead, you've done nothing but hold it against me."

Paul states his intention to visit them again soon, stressing that his fatherly relationship with them makes it imperative that this visit be on the same terms as his previous ones—without pay (12:14). His love for them spills over into loving service (12:15a). The rhetorical question in 12:15b, "If I love you too much, will I be loved the less for that?" is more pathetic than sarcastic. Apparently some of the Corinthians (probably at the urging of the false apostles) had claimed that his rejection of financial support was merely a ruse to make them that much more indebted to him. The memory of this charge (perhaps along with a charge of financial dishonesty in receiving payoffs from his helpers) still rankles Paul, and he vigorously refutes it by pointing to the guilelessness of his own conduct and that of his delegates (12:16-18).

Paul's bitter question at the beginning of 12:19 reflects the resentment he felt at being forced into the absurd position of having to defend himself. He swears that God, at least, knows the purity of his motives (12:19b). Then he shares with them his very real concern over the outcome of his proposed visit (12:20-21). He is afraid that some of the Corinthians might not have changed all that much, that they might still be into the same old sins as before. He expresses himself in a threatening way hoping that the threat of his presence will coerce them into repentance. There is a warning of excommunication in 12:21, since the Church "mourned" the loss of those whom it had to expel because of continuing in serious sin.

Quoting from Deuteronomy 19:15, which concerns the number of witnesses needed to sustain a verdict of guilty, Paul uses this text in the context of his visits to Corinth: if he comes again and still finds them in sin, he will have enough evidence to take serious action, and take serious action he will (13:1-2). He is speaking sarcastically in 13:3, probably throwing back at the false apostles and their friends a saying of theirs to the effect that Paul is weak but they are strong, and taunting him to show them his power if he is such a great apostle. Paul tells them that if he comes and has to resort to severe discipline, they will simply be getting what they asked for—a demonstration of his power.

He draws an analogy between his own ministry and the ministry of Jesus in 13:4—just as Jesus appeared to be weak, but God raised him up, so too Paul appears to be weak in Jesus, but God establishes him as well. The clear hint is that they had better watch out with whom they are tangling! He serves a double challenge in 13:5, asking them to "test" and "examine" themselves (as a smithy tries iron) to see if they really are in relationship with Jesus Christ. As for himself, he confidently implies that everything he does can stand the "test" of his relationship with Christ (13:6). Even though it may cost him a show of power, he sincerely hopes that those who need to will come to their senses and repent so that he will not have to use his God-given authority in a negative way (13:7-10).

Paul closes this most passionate of all his letters with a final exhortation to perfection (the "Mend your ways" of the NAB is rather weak here), communal encouragement, unity, and the well-being that comes with peace—God's presence will be with them if they take their calling seriously in this way (13:11). His invitation to exchange the kiss of peace (13:12) is his way of sharing this significant gesture with them in the context of a letter. The final benediction (13:13) is the most developed of any in his letters. It is notable because it assumes a vital communion (a kind of Communion of Saints!) between Christ, God, and the Holy Spirit while at the same time acknowledging them as individual persons. It is one of the clearest hints of the coming doctrine of the Trinity which we have in the New Testament.

Questions for Personal Reflection/Group Discussion:

1. Do you think Paul's extensive use of boasting in chapters 10-13 is an acceptable or unacceptable way to make a point? Why?
2. (a) What was the lesson that Paul learned from his weakness, or handicap, that would not go away?
   (b) Do you have to bear such a "cross" or disappointment in your own life?
   (c) How might it be a source of strength rather than weakness?

Epilogue

Apparently Paul's passionate letter (II Corinthians) did achieve its hoped-for result of reconciliation between him and the Corinthians. We know from the letter to the Romans (Rm 15:25-26) that he did indeed take a substantial gift to Jerusalem, and that for this gift to be substantial he would have had to have achieved reconciliation with the Corinthians. Indeed, the reconciliation was completed in person, as Paul was able to return to Corinth and spend three months with the church there (Acts 20:1-3a). This visit must have been a positive and productive one, for it was during this time that he wrote his letter to the Romans, his great treatise on Christian faith.

II Corinthians is the last of Paul's early letters. Its completion marked a turning point in his "literary" life. As we shall see in a subsequent volume, *St. Paul's Later Letters: faith, compassion, mystery, community, joy,* Paul regroups his theological forces in his letter to the Romans (faith), pleads for mercy for a fellow Christian in his letter to Philemon (compassion), considers the mystical dimension of the Christian life in his letters to the Colossians and Ephesians (mystery), examines the most appropriate form of organization for the Church in I & II Timothy and Titus (community) and, finally, reflects on the exhilarating depths of his life as a Christian in his letter to the Philippians (joy).